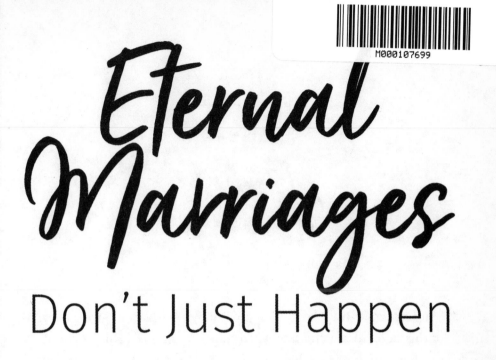

Eternal Marriages

Don't Just Happen

Praise for

Eternal Marriages

Don't Just Happen

"An important read for all married couples—I plan to give a copy of this book to my children when they get engaged. Shields covers the hard topics from his perspective as a divorce attorney and applies gospel understanding garnered from a lifetime of study. As a father with cancer Shields has compiled what he considers most meaningful for the benefit of children he may not be able to counsel throughout their married lives. The principles he shares will ring true to all married couples."

—LISA RATY, designer for White Elegance and former owner of Candlelight Dresses

Eternal Marriages

Don't Just Happen

How to Avoid the 10 Most Common Pitfalls
on the Path to Happily Ever After

Mark A. Shields

CFI

An imprint of Cedar Fort, Inc.
Springville, Utah

ISBN 13: 978-1-4621-2241-7

Published by CFI, an imprint of Cedar Fort, Inc.
2373 W. 700 S., Springville, UT 84663
Distributed by Cedar Fort, Inc., www.cedarfort.com

LIBRARY OF CONGRESS CATALOGING-IN-PUBLICATION DATA

Names: Shields, Mark A. (Mark Alan), author.
Title: Eternal marriages don't just happen : how to avoid the 10 most common
  dangers on the path to happily ever after / Mark Shields.
Description: Springville, Utah : CFI, An imprint of Cedar Fort, Inc., [2018]
  | Includes bibliographical references and index.
Identifiers: LCCN 2018006759 (print) | LCCN 2018010925 (ebook) | ISBN
  9781462129164 (epub, pdf, mobi) | ISBN 9781462122417 (perfect bound : alk.
  paper)
Subjects: LCSH: Marriage--Religious aspects--Church of Jesus Christ of
  Latter-day Saints. | Marriage--Religious aspects--Mormon Church. | Marital
  quality.
Classification: LCC BX8643.M36 (ebook) | LCC BX8643.M36 S55 2018 (print) |
  DDC 248.8/44--dc23
LC record available at https://lccn.loc.gov/2018006759

Cover design by Jeff Harvey
Cover design © 2018 Cedar Fort, Inc.
Edited by Hali Bird and Justin Greer
Typeset by Kaitlin Barwick

Printed in the United States of America

10 9 8 7 6 5 4 3 2 1

Printed on acid-free paper

Also by

MARK A. SHIELDS

Your Endowment

Your Covenant

*Gospel Symbols: Finding the
Creator in His Creations*

*Holy Gifts: The True Meaning of
Gold, Frankincense & Myrrh*

*Discoveries in Chiasmus:
A Pattern in All Things*

CONTENTS

CONTENTS

INTRODUCTION

My wife, Cami, and I have been married twenty-five years. She is truly a gem. She is absolutely wonderful and is ahead of me in just about every way imaginable. I love her dearly.

I have spent more than twenty of those years as a divorce lawyer. That means I represent people in all sorts of difficult situations regarding marriages—failed marriages, specifically—and all things related to them, including custody battles, support battles, and property battles. That also means I see everything that goes wrong in a marriage and ultimately kills the marriage.

Most of those years with Cami have been spent raising our five daughters. They are without question beautiful, unique, and just plain awesome. I would do anything for them.

The last five years have been spent with a diagnosis of late-stage cancer. It's an incurable disease that, statistically speaking, should have killed me a few years ago.

With the help of that disease, I have learned something that relates heavily to the twenty-five years with Cami, the twenty plus years practicing family law, and the twenty-three plus years as a father of daughters. This is something that I'm sure I knew before I even came to this earth, as if the veil had been removed. What is this great lesson I have learned? I have learned that I

1

would give anything and everything I have for my daughters to be blessed with good, righteous, loving husbands. Really, there is nothing else in this world that truly matters to me. That's it. With the blessing of a strong marriage for each of my daughters, I would consider myself the luckiest man on the face of the earth, even with this disease that could be considered so terrible.

As I write this, I feel a little like King Benjamin. I am gathering loved ones in my old age, so to speak, and I am sharing with my family and all of you dear readers this extremely important message with all the energy of my soul. The process of learning the lessons I'm going to share has cost me dearly, as I've spent my sanity in a profession filled with fighting, ugliness, and things gone wrong. I know full well that this message can help many, many people have a happy marriage that puts them well on the way to the greatest blessings that our Father in Heaven has for them. Lehi must have felt the same way when he gathered his posterity (2 Nephi 4). And I'm sure Adam felt the same way when he "was bowed down with age, being full of the Holy Ghost" (D&C 107:56) and left a blessing on his posterity.

I don't mind telling you that I've tried to write this book several times over the last six years or so. Each time I've started, I've backed off, mostly because I felt unworthy to be talking about great marriages. It's true—happy marriages don't just happen. You see, marriage can be hard. It's not 72 degrees and sunny with blue skies, a light wind, and happy, beautiful music playing in the background all day. It's hard work. Many times, that hard work has kept me from physically writing this book that has been prewritten in my head for years, because I didn't want to feel like a hypocrite. Well, I'm now embracing the hard parts in the hope that I can help some of you get on the path to happily ever after and stay on that path, come what may.

I don't mean to be melodramatic talking about my condition because, much like a Monty Python character, I'm not dead yet. I just have what I believe is a unique perspective as a father of five daughters, a new grandfather, a stage-four cancer survivor, and a divorce lawyer. It means a whole lot to me to be able to share this perspective when I know without question that my life has been spared to this point to be able to share it with you.

I want my children, my grandchildren, and all of you to thrive in a happy marriage! I want you all to avoid the problems that I've seen turn something as beautiful as marriage into a miserable experience for so many people. I want you all to learn from the bad that I've seen and lived through as a lawyer. And I have every reason to believe you and your families will be blessed and will learn from these messages.

> *"Butterflies and zebras and moonbeams and fairy tales."*
>
> —Jimi Hendrix

We are brought up to love and appreciate beautiful and magical things and to believe in fairy tales. It comes naturally to us as children, before we get caught up in things like school, bills, and (gasp) responsibility.

Have you ever noticed how many fairy tales end with the prince and princess living happily ever after? Of course you have. Then you have no doubt also noticed that there's always something in the way of the prince and princess living happily ever after. Some evil threat—usually a villain—always tries to ruin the fairy tale and keep our lovebird heroes apart before they can reach that happily-ever-after point.

Well, I have somehow become an expert on those threats to happily ever after. It's an ugly business, to be sure. It takes a tremendous toll, especially when you care deeply and your clients become your friends as you struggle through traumatic trials with them. When people's quests for happily ever after do not end well, I end up with a bird's eye view of the villains that swoop in and ruin the happily ever after. Through well over a thousand cases—many of which have been LDS divorces—I have learned far too much about these villains that kill a marriage.

Think about it—if you can avoid these problems or villains, then your marriage can be everything you always dreamed it would be! Well, if I can help anyone avoid the pitfalls that bring marriages crashing down, then this is the best batch of lemonade I can possibly make from a career in a lemon grove. This book is my attempt to help as many people as possible avoid the most common things that rob marriages of their happiness.

"Everybody loves a happy ending."

—Tears for Fears

The Goal

The goal of this book is twofold:

1. Answer questions about the problems and pitfalls that lead to miserable and ultimately deceased marriages and the insurance against those problems.
2. Discuss the doctrinal bases for the common problems (where they apply) so that you can
    a. Recognize the threats.

  b. Avoid the threats.
  c. Make corrections to dig out of the threats.
  d. Teach others (most importantly, your children) to avoid the threats.

What You Need to Understand about the Symbols Used in This Book

Keeping with the fairy tale theme, much of this book will unfold like an allegory—a big parable that teaches lessons on eternity and marriage through the symbolism of fairy tales and threats. To understand this symbolism as you read, there are a few things in particular that you need to understand.

1. Marriage is not happily ever after; eternity is happily ever after.

I hate to shatter your dreams, but marriage itself here on earth is not happily ever after; it is the *path* to happily ever after. Think about it—the words *ever after* really mean eternity, don't they? Consider also that the fairy tales are about princes and princesses, not kings and queens. A prince and a princess are a future king and a future queen. They haven't reached the throne yet. Their future, not their present, is the true highlight of their lives. Mortality is barely the blink of an eye compared to eternity. Eternity is where the greatest blessings are to be found. As my friend Norma Smiley says, "Live for the blessings that eternity has yet to bestow on you."

Marriage works the same way as mortality itself. It is the perfect proving ground for us to develop the attributes that will most help us in eternity, but it is only a tiny thread in the endless fabric of eternity. The pathway there, just like life itself, is filled with trials, heartaches, countless bills to pay, errands to run, and all sorts of other challenges with each and every day. It's tough. It never goes as planned, but it is designed to be that way and to prepare us for even greater blessings. You spend mortality—that journey down the pathway—preparing yourself for eternity. You have to earn the blessing of eternal companionship.

Marriage is not a destination; it is a journey.

Think of it this way—marriage is not a destination; it is a journey. That journey is the only way to prepare us and make us worthy of happily ever after.

As a bonus, the same principles and counsel that lead you to happily ever after in the celestial kingdom will bring you glimpses of that happily ever after here in mortality! That means the same things that will you get you to happily ever after will also make your journey there magnificent—and happy.

2. The villains and other obstacles are collectively referred to as "threats."

In reality, marriage has a whole lot more than one villain, and those villains aren't just people. For our purposes in this book, those villains may also take the form of dangerous animals lurking on the path. They may be hidden traps. They may be lots of different things. In this book, we will refer to all of these things simply as "threats." This is where you will see that happy marriages don't just happen. You have to dodge these threats along the way to be happy. You have to get past these threats altogether to find ultimate happiness.

3. This book is designed to help you avoid those threats.

Think of this book as a guidebook to help you navigate around those threats and get to the dream castle (think the celestial kingdom) where you can live happily ever after. You could also think of this book as an abbreviated "for dummies" guidebook that focuses on the dangerous animals and conditions that are sure to find you at one point or another on this journey.

4. The Savior is your Guide on this journey.

Such an adventure to the castle of happily ever after most definitely requires a guide. No, this book is not that guide; the Savior is the Guide.

5. The scriptures and inspired teachings of the Lord's servants are the map.

Such an adventure also requires a map. The scriptures and inspired words of Church leaders—the Guide's helpers—are the map.

Throughout all of this, remember—a strong marriage is the greatest source of happiness here on earth and throughout the eternities. That is a promise from our Heavenly Father, and His promises are sure. With that promise, you can rest assured that you will have a great experience on the adventure that is marriage and in the eternal destination it leads you to . . . as long as you don't fall prey along the way. Those dangers can make a bad marriage feel like a prison sentence, even though marriage is designed to give the greatest mortal joy possible in the Plan of Salvation and a happily ever after in the eternities.

Here's to avoiding the bad so we can relish the good and reach the eternal happily ever after.

Note: As both a lawyer and an author, I am used to citing chapter and verse for every point I make. If you are similarly used to seeing a scripture, a statute, or a Supreme Court case cited for each point, please know that I can't do that in this book. I can't compromise my clients or anyone else by citing them individually as the experiences. That wouldn't be fair to them, and I assure them that I am not pointing to their case in any isolated or specific way. Even if their stories came out in a courtroom, where everything is public record and may not be technically confidential, they are still personal and deeply emotional.

I respect that and want to keep respecting that. This book is not about individuals; it's about trends and themes. As I said, no confidences will be broken. I am convinced that the messages I have to share in this book can help many, many people avoid the marriage mortician and make it happily ever after. (*Marriage mortician* is what I'll call a divorce lawyer. We divorce lawyers have earned the right to such self-deprecation.)

Here we go!

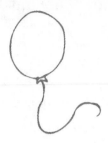

Questions and Answers about the Journey to Happily Ever After

Q: What are the most common pitfalls you see in marriages?

A: That is such a good question that it gets the biggest section of this book.

Here are your quick answers, the most wanted villains:

1. Selfishness
2. Midlife crises
3. Forgetting covenants
4. Self-righteousness
5. Sexual issues
6. Pornography
7. Debt
8. Abuse
9. Adultery
10. Untreated mental health issues

Q: Are those listed in any particular order?

A: Roughly.

They are listed roughly in order from most frequent to least common. It's not a scientific ranking system, so don't get too hung up thinking one is less dangerous than another. Each of these problems can be fatal to a marriage, with debt or midlife crises probably being the most conquerable for various reasons. Physical abuse is probably the single most fatal poison in a marriage, but I'm happy—or more like *grateful*—to report that it is relatively rare in my experience.

Q: What is the single best piece of advice you can give for a happy marriage?

A: This one is a piece of cake. Attend the temple worthily and regularly.

There is no such thing as an unhappy couple who regularly and worthily attends the temple. I repeat, there is no such thing as an unhappy couple who regularly and worthily attends the temple.

As a bishop, whenever a couple came to me with struggles, I always asked them, "When was the last time you went to the temple together?" I already knew the answer to the question. I didn't ask the question for my benefit or understanding; I asked it for their benefit and understanding. Without exception, the answer was, "Well . . . a long time ago." Some people couldn't even remember when, it had been so long.

Others attended the temple separately. There's no doubt that worthy temple attendance by any measure is a good thing, but something very real and powerful unites a couple when they attend together. In some cases, one spouse will not be part of the equation because of worthiness concerns. In other cases, the spouses are just not aligned. They don't view the temple experience in the same way, or they just don't make it a priority. Whatever the case, friends, don't miss out on these blessings! Don't restrict yourselves to only half a blessing when a full and complete blessing is waiting for you by being worthy and attending the temple together.

It's no coincidence that so many temples look like castles or fairy-tale palaces. The Hebrew word for "temple" actually *means* "palace," and a palace is where royalty resides. That's definitely no coincidence. If you want to end up in a happily-ever-after palace, spend as much time as you can in the temple.

If you're looking for one single magic bullet in marriage, this is it. Nothing infuses a marriage with the presence of the Holy Ghost and with a spirit of happiness like temple attendance. It is the best rehearsal and preparation for eternity that exists.

Q: What do you mean by "regularly," as in "regularly attend the temple"?

A: As often as your circumstances permit.

That's the best answer I can give. (Actually, it's not my answer; it comes from Lesson 7 of *Endowed from on High,* the Church's temple prep manual.) The Brethren have made it a point not to put a quota on temple attendance, just as they have made it a point not to keep specific records of who attends and how often. On this subject, it strongly appears that the Lord wants us to make our temple attendance a very personal issue and an equally personal decision.

But let me put the issue in another light, to help you make that personal decision. How often do you eat? How often do you drink water? How often do you fill up your car with gasoline?

11

How often do you pay your bills? How often do you *breathe*? Well, if we don't do those things *regularly*, things go downhill quickly. We get hungry, thirsty, and eventually malnourished. We run out of gas and get stranded. We lose electricity, water, or our house. So, when we think of *regular* temple attendance, there are lessons to be learned from these worldly activities.

Q: What do you mean by "worthily" attend the temple?

A: Being able to answer the temple recommend interview questions properly at all times.

The temple recommend interview questions should be a constant part of our thought process. Chastity, tithing, sustaining our leaders—we know the questions. Living our lives with them in mind is, I believe, a huge part of what it means to remember the Savior always, as we covenant to do each time we take the sacrament.

When we need to make course corrections to bring ourselves into harmony with the temple recommend questions, let's do it, promptly and thoroughly. It's as simple as that.

In his first address in General Conference after being called as the President of the Church, President Howard W. Hunter wasted no time in pleading with members of the Church: "It is the deepest desire of my heart to have every member of the Church worthy to enter the temple. It would please the Lord if every adult member would be worthy of—and carry—a current temple recommend. The things that we must do and not do to be worthy of a temple recommend are the very things that ensure we will be happy as individuals and as families" ("Exceeding Great and Precious Promises," *Ensign*, November 1994). These words still apply today, and they cannot be overstated. The worthiness requirements of a temple recommend "are the very things that ensure we will be happy as individuals and as families."

Q: We hear so much about things like pornography. We know it is a serious worthiness problem. Is there a particular aspect of worthiness that doesn't get as much mention and might be overlooked?

A: As a matter of fact, there is.

Let me suggest one of the more underappreciated questions of particular importance in our continued worthiness to attend the temple. In outlining the qualifications to enter the temple, Elder Robert D. Hales included the question, "Is there anything in your conduct relating to members of your family that is not in harmony with the teachings of the Church?" ("Preparing for a Heavenly Marriage," *Ensign*, February 2006). In other words, are you a good husband? Are you a good wife? Are you a good father/mother? Are you a good son/daughter? In my experience, this is a painfully underappreciated question.

If you yell at people in your family, it should affect the way you answer this question as you ponder it each day.

If you hold grudges or harbor bad feelings against someone in your family, it definitely should impact your answer to this question—*especially* when you believe it's the other person's fault.

If you engage in any level of physical or sexual abuse within marriage, you cannot answer this question in a way that qualifies you for a recommend.

The temple recommend questions should not just come up every other year when we renew our recommends; they need to be constantly on our minds and in our hearts. This question in particular deserves more introspective attention and honesty in our everyday lives than we probably give it.

If your temple recommend is truly your prized possession, as President Hunter taught that it should be, then nothing is worth risking that recommend.

Q: Aren't you oversimplifying? Can temple attendance really help a marriage that much?

A: No, I am not oversimplifying. It really is that important and that powerful.

I make no secret that I love the temple and that I have dedicated myself to helping people understand, appreciate, and love the temple. The power of the temple is so real, tangible, and overwhelming that most people have barely scratched the surface of the blessings the temple offers. The temple is literally where heaven meets earth. If we are to invite a piece (or the peace) of heaven into our homes, the temple is where we will find it. There is no other experience in this world that walks us from one end of eternity to the other like the temple. In the temple, we symbolically walk back to the presence of God. Then, when we finish that experience, we walk back to our homes. Clouds of glory inevitably follow us from the temple to the home.

The laws, ordinances, and covenants of the temple are the same laws and covenants of a happy marriage. Think about that for a minute. The very laws we must obey in order to return to God are the same laws that will bring us happiness in marriage. Regular temple attendance keeps those laws fresh in our minds and hearts, just as the sacrament is intended to do each week.

I can make this promise with more confidence than any other promise I could give you. Be worthy of your temple recommend. Use it regularly. Use it together. There is not a single disadvantage to this formula. Only blessings will come. Nothing will insulate you from the marriage mortician like regular, worthy temple attendance.

And you don't have to take my word for it. Prophets, seers, revelators, and special servants of the Savior Jesus Christ will tell you the same thing.

✦ **Sister Jean B. Bingham, Relief Society General President:** "As we persevere and attend the temple, we'll have the Savior's help to overcome the world in which we live. One time as my husband and I were preparing to leave for the temple, one problem after another cropped up. Finally, as we were nearly out the door, we had a strained 'marital moment.' As the two of us walked silently to the car, we could hear our oldest daughter reassure her sister, 'Don't worry; they always come home happy from the temple.' And she was right!" ("The Temple Gives Us Higher Vision," *Ensign,* January 2018)

✦ **President Thomas S. Monson:** "As we attend the temple, there can come to us a dimension of spirituality and a feeling of peace which will transcend any other feeling which could come into the human heart. We will grasp the true meaning of the words of the Savior when He said: 'Peace I leave with you, my peace I give unto you . . . Let not your heart be troubled, neither let it be afraid.'

"My brothers and sisters, in our lives we will have temptations; we will have trials and challenges. As we go to the temple, as we remember the covenants we make there, we will be better able to overcome those temptations and to bear our trials. In the temple we can find peace." ("Blessings of the Temple," *Ensign,* May 2015)

✦ **President Gordon B. Hinckley:** "I make you a promise that if you will go to the house of the Lord, you will be blessed, life will be better for you . . . we will be a better people, we will be better fathers and husbands, we will be better wives and mothers." ("Excerpts from Recent Addresses of President Gordon B. Hinckley," *Ensign,* July 1997)

✦ "You'll leave the temple better than you arrived. I promise." (*Deseret News*, November 14, 2002)

✦ "Something will happen to you when you do [temple work]. I make you a promise that every time you go to the temple, you will leave a better man or woman than you were when you went inside the doors of the temple." (*Church News*, July 2, 2005)

✦ **President Ezra Taft Benson:** "Now let me say something else to all who can worthily go to the House of the Lord. When you attend the temple and perform the ordinances that pertain to the House of the Lord, certain blessings will come to you:

- You will receive the spirit of Elijah, which will turn your hearts to your spouse, to your children, and to your forebears.

- You will love your family with a deeper love than you have loved before.

- Your hearts will be turned to your fathers and theirs to you.

- You will be endowed with power from on high as the Lord has promised.

- You will receive the key of the knowledge of God (D&C 84:19). You will learn how you can be like Him. Even the power of godliness will be manifest to you (D&C 84:20).

- You will be doing a great service to those who have passed to the other side of the veil in order that they might be "judged according to men in the flesh, but live according to God in the spirit" (D&C 138:34).

Such are the blessings of the temple and the blessings of frequently attending the temple." ("What I Hope You Teach Your Children about the Temple," *Ensign,* August 1985)

✦ **Elder Boyd K. Packer:** "No work is more of a protection to this Church than temple work and the genealogical research which supports it. No work is more spiritually refining. No work we do gives us more power. No work requires a higher standard of righteousness. Our labors in the temple cover us with a shield and a protection, both individually and as a people." (*The Holy Temple,* 265)

"The veil is drawn back a little more. Our knowledge and vision of the eternities expands. It is always refreshing." (*The Holy Temple,* 39)

✦ **Elder Vaughn J. Featherstone:** "I promise you that all who faithfully attend to temple work will be blessed beyond measure. Your families will draw closer to the Lord, unseen angels will watch over your loved ones when Satanic forces tempt them, the veil will be thin and great spiritual experiences will distill upon this people." (Address given at the Mount Vernon Washington Stake Conference, June 1985)

You see, this is not just my promise; it is the promise from the Lord's anointed. I am only putting these promises directly into the context of a happy marriage.

I repeat: There is no such thing as an unhappy couple who regularly and worthily attends the temple.

Q: What is the second-best piece of
   advice for a happy marriage?

A: Be as likeable and as easy to get
   along with as humanly possible.

Being worthy of a temple recommend is huge, but not every marriage problem is a product of worthiness. It's still very possible to be worthy but also, well, annoying. It's possible to be worthy but not be a great or fun spouse. There are plenty of people who are pillars of righteousness but are not necessarily easy to get along with or fun to be around. In addition to being worthy of using that recommend, we really do need to try each day to be very easy people to get along with. We probably all know righteous and good people who have been divorced or who have been stuck in unhappy marriages. I'm certainly not going to jump to the conclusion that their spouses are all evil and presume that's the reason why their marriages failed or limped along; I'm just saying that being likeable is about more than being righteous. It's a skill.

Think of it this way—the Church has invested hugely in missionary training centers. Those centers don't just preach to missionaries that they need to be perfectly righteous and great results will automatically flow. Obedience and faith are certainly the core principles of any successful missionary, but there are other qualities—other *skills*, for lack of a better word—that are essential. "Remember faith, virtue, knowledge, temperance, patience, brotherly kindness, godliness, charity, humility, diligence" (D&C 4:6). For lack of a better umbrella term, I am summarizing these words and skills in the context of marriage with the word *likeable*.

You know these qualities as the essential characteristics of a successful missionary. They also happen to be the essential characteristics of a successful spouse, a likeable spouse. Putting those characteristics into practice in everyday marriage is a skill.

There are a few necessary steps to develop skills. First, you have to want to develop the skill. Second, you have to practice the skill. Some of these qualities/skills are needed every day of a marriage. At a minimum, kindness, faith, and patience are needed every day, if not several times a day. Charity, humility, diligence: they all are necessary attributes and skills to be practiced throughout marriage as well. The ability to avoid overreacting is most definitely a helpful marriage skill. It involves kindness, patience, humility, and probably other skills. My wife will let you know when I've learned that skill. Together, these skills make you a very likeable spouse.

To help us understand both righteousness and likeability in a spouse, we are going to learn some lessons from trees. Yes, trees. Stick with me just a little bit and it will make sense.

Trees are used as scriptural symbols of righteous people (Psalms 1:1–4). For our purposes, we are expanding this to mean not just righteous spouses but *successful* spouses. A fully mature tree can live to be hundreds of years old, standing the test of time and growing more and more majestic through that test. That sounds a lot like a successful marriage. Each year brings seasons of intense cold, scorching heat, fierce winds, hard rains, and spells of drought with no rain at all. Through these never-ending cycles, the trees keep right on growing. In marriage, there is no calendar for these storms. A marriage might even hit a bitterly cold deep freeze in July. An acid rain downpour can pop up in the middle of a perfect day, and an earthquake might even hit in the middle of a long drought. It takes a special kind of tree to withstand weather like this, yet a good marriage will only grow stronger through this weather.

A mature tree blesses people with shade and fruit. A successful marriage blesses family and friends and brings forth fruit in the form of righteous posterity. And the fruit remains to bless generations to come.

How does a tree survive storms like this? Different trees do it in different ways. Most trees survive because they have exceptional root structures. An olive tree can live for 2,000 years. That means some of the same olive trees of the Savior's time are still alive today! A big reason for this is that their roots grow so intricately that they invade the surrounding ground, bringing up sprouts all around.

A giant redwood sports a root system that only goes 5 or 6 feet deep but extends up to 100 feet from the tree itself. Redwoods have been known to live over 2,000 years. Giant redwoods are the tallest trees in the world. In the same class as a redwood, a sequoia's roots go deeper, about 12 to 14 feet, and even wider, covering a full acre and over 90,000 cubic feet of soil. The oldest living sequoia tree is an astounding 3,266 years old. Sequoias and giant redwoods are the trees that tower to the heavens. Tourists come from all over the globe just to see these trees. They are incredible, and their root systems get most of the credit. They stabilize them through any storm and bring in nutrients constantly to feed the giants.

You get the picture. Roots play a huge role in a tree's survival, growth, and ability to thrive.

In the forty or so years I've lived in Arizona, I've seen countless trees leveled by the surprisingly vicious monsoon storms that hit our desert each year. It seems like every storm, even the average ones, will bring down trees somewhere on the way to or from work.

But in all those years, I don't think I have ever seen a single palm tree downed by one of these storms. And there are palm trees everywhere.

How do palm trees survive? Well, in this case, it's not their root systems. Their root systems are so small that they barely extend beyond the tree trunk and only go a few feet deep. This completely defies the lessons about these other trees and their secrets to long-term survival and thriving. Palm trees go about the survival and growth process in a completely different way. They are extremely *flexible*. (Think: not easily offended, likeable, easygoing.) They're sleek and aerodynamic. They don't give those storms a whole lot to grab onto. They make it through the storms by bending and letting the storms go right past them.

Flexibility, especially in the context of marriage, is a skill. It requires temperance, patience, kindness, humility, and plenty of the other skills from section 4 of the Doctrine and Covenants that apply to successful spouses.

"As you wish."

—Westley, *The Princess Bride*

Both of these survival/thriving strategies—hearty roots and flexibility—are great lessons on marriage.

Think of the root structure as righteousness. Our roots grow deep in the gospel. The parable of the sower compares people's spiritual growth to seeds taking root (Matthew 13:3–23; Mark 4:3–21; Luke 8:5–15). A foundation in Christ is the only sure foundation that will never give way in a storm (Helaman 5:12; Matthew 5:24–29).

But strong root systems don't grow overnight. They can take years and decades to grow strong enough to keep up with the rest of the tree. And strong roots by themselves won't get us through every storm. Remember, even trees with seemingly solid root structures can be taken down in storms, just as even righteous people can have unhappy marriages.

While we are growing our foundational roots over the course of many, many years, we need to take lessons from palm trees as well, bending and adapting (read: forgiving) to the weather conditions and to our spouse's needs.

So, in trees, we see lessons on righteousness (root structure/ foundation), likeability (flexibility), and mercy. My friends, when storms hit, be like a tree, whichever tree you need to be like.

Q: You mention flexibility and likability as skills. What is another skill needed in a good marriage?

A: Communication, with an emphasis on listening to understand.

Communication is a skill that divorcing couples lack or have just plain lost. The ability to communicate well, especially in marriage, depends mostly on being a good listener. So many problems in marriage arise because spouses listen to each other with the goal of *responding* to what is said. We want to be able to sound like we know what we're talking about, or we want to be able to defend ourselves when something critical is said about us. We are anxious for the other person to finish the sentence so that we can chime in with our two cents or hit back.

What spouses really need is the ability to listen with the goal of *understanding* what is said. If you can learn to listen to understand—to get a real picture not just of what your spouse is saying but why he or she is saying it—then you will be an effective communicator in marriage. Many times, your spouse just wants to know you care. When you spend your listening time getting ready to defend yourself or impress someone in response, you too often miss what is really being communicated. Notice I said what is really being *communicated* and not what is being *said*. There is a difference.

Let me give you an example. When my wife and I were in grad school, there was this three-year-old boy in our complex about the same age as our oldest child. He had his own little language, and it was really quite cool. It emphasized a lot of grunting r-sounds, kind of like the Swedish Chef on the Muppets. One time he got a hold of the microphone in sacrament meeting and let it rip. It was just awesome. It was a pure joy to hear him trying to talk. The problem was, everybody spoke back to him in this obviously foreign language we call English. He had to feel like everybody was so intent on redirecting him, even if it was well intentioned, but he just wanted someone to try to understand him.

Well, one day I was in nursery with him when he started holding court. As he started his monologue, he sort of gravitated toward me. Having studied a few foreign languages and having watched more than a few Muppet episodes back in the day, I decided to try my hand at speaking back with him. I knelt down, looked him straight in the eye, and gave it my best. He stared at me. Just stared for at least a few seconds. His jaw dropped. He had this look of wonder and amazement in his eyes. Instead of saying anything back, he walked right up to me and gave me a big old hug. Finally, somebody spoke his language! Or at least tried. Every time I saw the little guy after that, he had an adorable smile for me, if not a hug. In just a few seconds, I had made a good friend. It wasn't because I responded to him; my words were pure gibberish, of course. It was because I listened to him and tried to understand him. *Then* I responded to him.

Spouses tend to have their own language. It won't be as unique as my little friend's, but it will not be straightforward English, either. Different words will mean different things, and those meanings will change in different contexts. To be on the same team and to be true friends, you will have to listen to understand what is truly being communicated. Only then can you give a response that shows that you really understand or at least that you tried to understand. (You generally do get spouse points for a sincere effort in marriage, even if you don't quite succeed.) You will have to learn what your spouse's love language is, and then you will have to learn that language. That's a skill. Learn it. Use it. It will help you immensely.

Q: Do men and women tend to have different problems?

A: Yes, but it's only a tendency.

It might be more accurate to state that men and women tend to show different symptoms of the same disease. For the most part, couples tend to fall into pitfalls together. When the problems are individual, I try to approach the subject from both husbands' and wives' perspectives.

Q: Do you notice a particular strategy that seems to be working for Satan right now?

A: Yes, definitely. He's going after wives and mothers with everything he has right now.

For the first several years of my practice, it was the men—the husbands and fathers—who were going off the deep end. The problems of pornography, leaving the Church, and various levels of being an all-around jerk were far more prevalent among men.

During those years, I had barely a handful of guys I would feel comfortable recommending to a girl. Over the last several years, that has changed, and it has changed in a big, big way. Now I see far fewer women in divorces whom I would feel comfortable recommending to someone. This trend has become so alarming and such a reversal from my previous experience that I have talked with other lawyers about it. They have noticed the same thing. Satan is going after mothers full-bore right now, and he is winning far too many of the battles.

His reasons are obvious. If he can get a man to stray, that's one man he has in his grasp. With the divine role that wives and mothers play, the stakes are higher. If he can get a woman to stray, that's too often an entire family he has led astray. Sisters, please understand and be aware that right now you are the adversary's prime target.

Q: What specifically is he doing to go after wives and mothers?

A: A lot of it starts with obsession over physical appearance and "success."

The adversary is getting a lot of mileage these days out of having women obsess over their bodies and their physical appearances. Actually, this isn't a new strategy at all; he's just taking down more people with it now than in times past. This emphasis on the temporal too often leads mothers away from the spiritual. Obsession in general takes time away from family. Time is spent at the gym when that time is sometimes sorely needed at the home. Time at the gym can lead to extra efforts to look good and make new acquaintances there, which has led to more than one affair.

Nobody seems to notice it while it's happening, but there is one other problem with gym obsessions that is often overlooked: Time at the gym is usually time without wearing the temple garment. Guards are let down, and the covenants symbolized by the temple garment are pushed away from the forefront. Temptations creep in, and the protection offered by our covenants is lost.

Now, don't get me wrong on this subject. I'm a marathon runner, and I credit fitness with preserving my life. I am a huge, huge advocate of fitness. It's not evil. It just has the potential to lead to problems when it pushes covenants out of the way.

I think maybe the problems with fitness obsessions come from the motivation behind the fitness. If you're doing it all so you'll look hot—especially if you're trying to impress someone other than your spouse—then I think you're getting into dangerous territory. You also have to be very careful and certain that your fitness efforts don't steal time, your heart, or your mind away from your family's needs. Like so much in life, I think it boils down to your heart. Where is it? If it's truly with your family, then I think your fitness bonanza can be a big blessing. If your heart is set on the way you look, the company at the gym, or something else, then it's time to make a course correction. Again, men can fall into the same trap quite easily. The trap just seems to be ensnaring more wives than husbands at present, in my experience.

Wives and mothers, these are not the only ways the adversary will go after you. Like King Benjamin, I can't list all the ways (Mosiah 4:29). "But this much I can tell you, that if ye do not watch yourselves, and your thoughts, and your words, and your deeds, and observe the commandments of God, and continue in the faith of what ye have heard concerning the coming of our Lord, even unto the end of your lives, ye must perish. And now, O [woman], remember, and perish not" (Mosiah 4:30).

Wives and mothers, please, please watch yourselves. Husbands too, of course, but especially you wives, because you appear to be Satan's most wanted right now, and because you are irreplaceable in the Plan of Salvation.

Q: What can we do on a daily basis to bring blessings into our marriage?

A: Read the scriptures and pray together. Every. Single. Day.

The single best piece of marriage advice my wife, Cami, and I ever got was when we were engaged. Cami's bishop challenged us to end every day reading scriptures together and then kneeling and praying together as a couple, holding hands. He challenged us to start right then and there while we were engaged. We started then and have never looked back. Yes, you can start this while you're engaged. When Cami and I were engaged, we would read and pray at Cami's house. I would then hop on my sleek, impressive Honda Aero 50 scooter and head back to my place. Once we got married, the whole process became easier. The Beach Boys were right—it really was that much better when we could say goodnight and stay together.

Reading and praying together every day isn't just a magic-wand solution, lest you think I am oversimplifying again. Here's why: This accomplishes so many things at the same time. First, it brings you together every day. You're not living separate lives. You are one. Take advantage of this time to hold hands and to be close. You can take turns rubbing each other's back. If it's your night to read, you get a back rub while you read. There is even more unity as you kneel together, holding hands to pray.

Second, it invites the Holy Ghost. The influence of the Spirit is a natural blessing of scripture study and prayer. Here, you both get that blessing at the same time.

Third, it gives you a prime opportunity to express love for each other. You are praying out loud together as a couple. There is a certain very real power about vocal prayers. When your spouse hears you praying specifically for him or her, you grow together. As you thank Heavenly Father for your spouse's goodness and triumphs of the day, you grow together. As you plead with Heavenly Father for your spouse's needs, you grow together even more. Some of the best advice I've heard is to let your children hear you pray for them specifically by name. Your spouse needs that same blessing at least as much as your children.

As you two are together, you have an opportunity to talk about your day or anything else on your mind. Warning—sometimes you're tired, and that's definitely not the right time to bring up deep or heavy subjects. Don't force a dramatic situation. That could backfire. But when you know you will be together at the end of each day (and I suppose you could start each day the same way), there will at least be an opportunity to talk.

Finally, let me suggest one other benefit of this daily habit: It can do wonders to improve your sex life. Hear me out. I have been amazed at how few people go to bed at the same time. While one spouse heads off to sleep, the other spouse is somewhere else in the house doing perhaps something important but more likely doing something worthless, like watching TV or playing video games. These same people complain about a lack of physical intimacy. If you're not physically, emotionally, or spiritually together, you can't have much of a hope for being physically intimate at the moment, can you? Reading and praying together each night may be a great place to start improving your sexual intimacy.

Q: Are there any magic words that can help a marriage?

A: Yes. The two most important words in the English language: *thank you.*

Failed marriages are full of people who see the bad in their spouse first and foremost. Sometimes, that's all they see. They get to the point where they are unable to give the other spouse credit for any good.

Here's how the magic works to avoid this negative tunnel vision of a spouse: When you express gratitude, you recognize the good in someone. You break out of the spiral of seeing the bad. You avoid the sadness where that spiral takes you.

"And in nothing doth man offend God, or against none is his wrath kindled, save those who confess not his hand in all things and obey not his commandments" (D&C 59:21). Ingratitude may be seen as a gateway sin. It invites pride, selfishness, and rebellion into our lives. These end up being dangerous and painful sins. It also leads you to that point where it's harder and harder to see the good in your spouse. Saying "thank you" goes a long way toward preventing these sad conditions.

"I want to thank you."

—Dido

We all need to be reminded of the good in people, and people certainly appreciate when others notice the good they do. Then, after we acknowledge the good in our spouse, it becomes easier and easier to see more and more good in the same spouse. And let's face it—being a parent and a spouse is often an incredibly thankless job. You have the power to change that, maybe not on your children's part or the world's part, but certainly on your part as a spouse.

Verbal expressions of gratitude are often priceless, especially to our sweethearts. I think of the words of a song based on the writings of a poet. "I've been through times when no one cared. I've seen clouds in empty skies, when one kind word meant more to me than all the love in paradise" ("To One in Paradise," The Alan Parsons Project, 1976). Making these two simple, kind words an everyday practice in your marriage will do wonders to keep you away from the marriage mortician. Not only will they bring some much-needed happiness to your spouse, they will keep you from the dreaded inability to see the good in your spouse that is part of the downward spiral of a failed marriage.

So far, our list of apparent magic wands now includes regular and worthy temple attendance, reading scriptures and praying together, and the two most important words in the English language: thank you.

Note: These and other "magic wands" such as prayer, scripture study, and family home evening don't work by eliminating problems. There will always be problems in life. Instead, these magic wands work by filling your lives with the Holy Ghost and with gratitude, humility, and togetherness. These blessings don't magically erase problems, although they do prevent a whole lot of problems. The real magic they work is found in giving you the ability, with the help of the Holy Ghost, humility, and the like, to solve your problems.

Second note: If the two most important words in the English language are "thank you," then "I'm sorry" can't be too far behind. Try it sometime. I think you'll like it. Your spouse surely will.

Q: What is the single most important gospel principle in a happy marriage?

A: Mercy.

Just about every question and every part of this book addresses a gospel principle, so there is no shortage of important principles that apply in a happy marriage. But I am going to answer this question by focusing on mercy. Hugh Nibley taught that all we can really do in life is repent and forgive. Brother Nibley was one of the most learned and brilliant men who ever walked the earth, yet his summary of the best things we can do in life was remarkably simple and not intellectually deep at all. Repent and forgive. I will summarize repentance and forgiveness by placing them under the umbrella of mercy.

So many marriages fail because of one or both spouses' inability to let go of something the other spouse did or failed to do. Spouses are human. That means that *all* spouses make plenty of mistakes. "For all have sinned, and come short of the glory of God" (Romans 3:23). That means that we all need to repent, and we all need to find forgiveness. In marriage, those sins that we all commit tend to remain on display to our spouses. They might see the best we do, but they too often see the worst of what we do. The only way to navigate through the inevitable mess-ups in life and marriage is to repent and forgive. We repent of our sins, and we forgive others' sins, especially our spouses'.

The Savior taught, "Blessed are the merciful: for they shall obtain mercy" (Matthew 5:7). There it is. If we want to obtain mercy, then we must give mercy. James echoes this principle. "For he shall have judgment without mercy, that hath shewed no mercy" (James 2:13). No one is exempt from the Lord's commandment to forgive (D&C 64:10). Family members should be the first ones to forgive and be forgiven.

As we cast judgment on anyone, especially our spouse, we have to remember the Lord's teaching/warning: "Judge not unrighteously, that ye be not judged: but judge righteous judgment. For with what judgment ye judge, ye shall be judged: and with what measure ye mete, it shall be measured to you again" (JST—Matthew 7:1–2). Once again, the Lord teaches that the mercy we show to others is the same mercy that will be shown to us.

And finally, on this subject, the Lord teaches in the Doctrine and Covenants, "Verily, verily, I say unto you, my servants, that inasmuch as you have forgiven one another your trespasses, even so I, the Lord, forgive you" (D&C 82:1). I think this scripture is particularly interesting because the Lord bestows the blessing in the present tense. The saints had forgiven each other. Because of this, the Lord actually and presently forgave them. "I, the Lord, forgive you." I love this because it is not just a promise of a future condition, it is forgiveness actually received in the present. That is a wonderful lesson on mercy, repentance, and forgiveness in marriage. It shows that mercy is available right here and now. It is a living doctrine from the Living Christ ready to be received today.

I have a painfully clear understanding of what kinds of sins I've committed through the years. That means I have a desperate and crucial need for mercy. If I am ever going to be forgiven of my sins so that I can walk back to the presence of God, I know I will need mercy of a magnitude that I can only hope and pray for. I am not alone in this need. Every person—that includes every husband and wife—has an infinite need of mercy. The only way to *receive* that level of mercy or forgiveness is to *show* that level of mercy or forgiveness to others. That necessarily starts with our spouse.

"Get over it."

—The Eagles

One of the quintessential marriage books is *The Peacegiver* by James L. Ferrell. The entire theme of this masterful work—basically a set of huge allegories—is the redeeming mercy available from the living Jesus Christ. His mercy is the ingredient to healing the broken hearts that litter broken marriages. The most moving and memorable lesson that I learned from *The Peacegiver* is to extend unending mercy to my wife because I have an unending need for mercy myself. If I expect or hope for mercy in the eternities—and we *all* need mercy infinitely—then I have to *give* mercy infinitely. We cannot receive forgiveness unless we forgive. Since any one of my sins would be enough to keep me from the presence and glory of God, I have to forgive every person who has trespassed against me. Literally **any sin unforgiven will keep me from the celestial kingdom.**

"Let it go. Surrender."

—U2

The family is the most indispensable starting point for mercy. Repent and forgive freely within marriage, of all places. You may think that you need mercy less than your spouse does. You're wrong. You both need it desperately since **one lone sin will keep you from the celestial kingdom** as much as one million sins will. You both need mercy, so you both must give mercy.

Don't keep score. That's for sports. Marriage isn't a sport. It's real life. Just repent and forgive completely.

Marriage's Greatest Threats: The Happily-Ever-After Killers

Keeping with our theme of the journey to happily ever after, these are the ten biggest dangers to look out for. If marriage is a big, beautiful, epic journey in a faraway land leading to a happily-ever-after eternity, then these are the villains, deadly animals, and traps on that journey. As you take in the beautiful sights on this adventure, remember to stay close to your Guide. He is the Savior. Remember to follow the map He has given us. It is the scriptures and the inspired words of the Guide's servants. With those reminders, here are the dangers to keep a distance from while on this most wonderful sojourn.

SELFISHNESS

There is one huge enemy to marriage that is woven throughout many if not all other pitfalls. President Spencer W. Kimball boiled every marriage failure down to one word: selfishness.

> Every divorce is the result of selfishness on the part of one or the other or both parties to a marriage contract. Someone is thinking of self—comforts, conveniences, freedoms, luxuries, or ease. Sometimes the ceaseless pinpricking of an unhappy, discontented, and selfish spouse can finally add up to serious physical violence. Sometimes people are goaded to the point where they erringly feel justified in doing the things which are so wrong. Nothing, of course, justifies sin. . . .
>
> The marriage that is based upon selfishness is almost certain to fail. The one who marries for wealth or the one who marries for prestige or social plane is certain to be disappointed. The one who marries to satisfy vanity and pride or who marries to spite or to show up another person is fooling only himself. But the one who marries to give happiness as well as receive it, to give service as well as to receive it, and who looks after the interests of the two and then the family as it comes will have a good chance that the marriage will be a happy one. (Spencer W. Kimball, *Marriage and Divorce* [Salt Lake City: Deseret Book, 1976], 19, 22)

I agree with President Kimball.

The two great commandments are to love the Lord first and your neighbor second (Matthew 22:37–39). Marriage is the ultimate forum to live these two great commandments, placing the Lord first and your neighbor (read: spouse) before yourself. This is an eternal lesson on priorities. If you keep the two great commandments, then you will be happy. If you don't, then you will be miserable, especially in marriage.

> *"Don't surround yourself with yourself."*
>
> —Yes

President James E. Faust also stressed the theme of unselfishness if a marriage is to succeed.

> There are a few simple, relevant questions that each person, whether married or contemplating marriage, should honestly ask himself. They are: (1) Am I able to think of the interest of my marriage and partner first, before I think of my own desires? (2) How deep is my commitment to my companion aside from any other interests? (3) Is he or she my best friend? (4) Do I have respect for the dignity of my partner as a person of worth and value? (5) Do we quarrel over money? (Money itself, or the lack of it, does not seem to make a couple either happy or unhappy, but it is often a symbol of selfishness.) (6) Is there a spiritually sanctifying bond between us? ("The Enriching of Marriage," *Ensign,* November 1977)

Selfishness or avoiding selfishness absolutely saturates these six themes raised by President Faust.

Perhaps this issue can be summed up by stating that a spouse who is truly ready to put the other spouse first is ready for a happy marriage.

"And if two can be one, who is the one two becomes?"

—Daryl Hall and John Oates

President Kimball also taught, "Two people coming from different backgrounds soon learn after the ceremony is performed that stark reality must be faced. There is no longer a life of fantasy or of make-believe; we must come out of the clouds and put our feet firmly on the earth. Responsibility must be assumed and new duties must be accepted. Some personal freedoms must be relinquished and many adjustments, unselfish adjustments, must be made" (*Marriage and Divorce*, 12–13).

These unselfish adjustments must be made again and again throughout marriage. Without these adjustments and a constant willingness to compromise, your marriage will consist of one spouse versus the other. You will never become one. And if you never become one, you will never be truly happy.

Think of it this way—Christian marriages are solemnized at an altar. That most definitely includes temple marriages. What is an altar? It is the place of sacrifice in the temple. Sacrifices were offered in the ancient temple on an altar, prefiguring the sacrifice of the Savior. *Your temple marriage is literally based and built on the principle and law of sacrifice.*

What are the sacrifices we offer in our marriage? To whom are those sacrifices offered? What do these sacrifices teach us about the Atonement? I will leave that to you to answer.

Consider also that the husband and wife both kneel at this altar in Christian marriages. What does kneeling represent? It shows humility, reverence, and submission. To whom? Again, I will leave that to you to ponder.

Whatever your answers, you cannot forget that your very marriage was solemnized at an altar that represents sacrifice, so your sealing is literally based on sacrifice. In any relationship based on the principle and law of sacrifice, you do not put yourself first. That is not how sacrifice works. Selfishness literally betrays the basis and foundation of your marriage.

Watch for selfishness cropping up throughout the pitfalls discussed here. Just don't look for it in others; look for it in yourself—of course.

Threat Level: The Big Bad Wolf

What do six of Aesop's Fables, three of Grimms' Fairy Tales, the English fairy tale of the "Three Little Pigs," the Russian musical tale "Peter and the Wolf," and a host of other TV and film tales all have in common? The Big Bad Wolf. He is probably the only villain who shows up in more than one fairy tale; I literally cannot count how many he's in. By this measure, the Big Bad Wolf is the most prolific or at least the most common villain out there, just like selfishness, as described by President Kimball.

It is important to note how selfishness provides this habitat for dangerous conditions. Like the Big Bad Wolf huffing and puffing, selfishness tears down instead of building up. When you seek to build up yourself instead of your spouse, you tear down your marriage. Take away selfishness, and the journey to happily ever after is much safer and far more enjoyable. Your house holds together much better. The other problems either stop growing, disappear altogether, or become much more manageable.

Q: If selfishness is the root in all these divorces, what can I do to avoid it on my part?

A: "Lord, is it I?"

When told that one of them would betray Him, the Savior's disciples asked, "Lord, is it I?" (Matthew 26:21–22). As President Dieter F. Uchtdorf pointed out, the disciples did not respond with, "Is it him?" ("Lord, Is It I?" *Ensign*, November 2014). From this experience, we learn that a true disciple of the Lord does not point fingers and blame others; a true disciple seeks first to make sure he or she is not the problem.

If your first thoughts when reading this book are about someone besides yourself, then you are missing the point. With each point of this book, you have to look first at yourself. Every last person has a fleck of dirt in his own eye, if not a full-fledged beam. Deal with that before you start looking at the mote in your spouse or potential spouse's eye (Matthew 7:3). An imperfect spouse cannot expect perfection from his or her spouse. When we discuss these problems, we have to ask ourselves constantly what *we* can do better. If we only think that others have problems, then we are guilty of the most common pitfall of all: selfishness. The best way I know of to avoid this pitfall, this Big Bad Wolf that haunts so many people's journey to happily ever after, is to ask ourselves constantly, "Lord, is it I?"

Midlife Crises

In my experience, midlife crises are probably the most common marriage fatality. Ironically, with a little work, they could also be the most survivable danger on our quest.

Q: What do you mean by "midlife crises"?

A: They take different forms. One is that people start looking for happiness outside of their marriage.

There is something strange that happens when people are in their forties. They examine their lives and decide that they're not happy with at least something in their lives. They realize that their lives are halfway over or more, and they want more out of life. These "crises" are very real and very natural. (Note: A midlife crisis can also occur earlier or later. This is just a generality.)

People start looking for happiness and fulfillment in different places, but those places far too often are outside of their own marriage. They don't look to their spouses as the source for happiness. They don't look to their covenants as the source for happiness. So, they start looking elsewhere. From there, spouses drift apart. Sometimes spouses change during this time and become very different—*too* different—from their former selves. That is not always a good thing.

Some people decide at this point that *things* can bring them happiness. (See the section on debt.) Well, the plan of salvation, appropriately called the plan of happiness also, is built on *people,* not things. A new motorcycle, sports car, or whatever it may be can definitely bring some happiness. It's just not going to be a lasting happiness. Then comes the reckoning that accompanies the new purchase when the individual can't make the payments on the new toy. That compounds the problem.

This does not have to be a fatal problem. You can work through this. You can straighten this out. Don't look at it as a "crisis"; look at it as an "adjustment." It can be a very positive thing.

I dealt with my receding hairline and expanding waistline by picking up running as a hobby. Since then, my age group in races has always been the most packed and competitive, so clearly lots of other people raised on '80s music are dealing with their crises in the same way.

At roughly the same age, and with some of our children in college, my wife went back to school to add a nursing degree to her family science degree. She has been fantastic at it and is a natural at caring for other people. This is a fantastic midlife adjustment. It's something she has wanted to do, and the time to do it has now presented itself. It has been a great outlet for her, and she has used it to develop her talents.

Whatever your outlet may be, my point is that a midlife adjustment can be a good thing. Remember, "The Family: A Proclamation to the World" stresses the importance of wholesome recreational activities. That could mean you take up hiking, wood carving, restoring furniture, fixing cars, or countless other things. If your midlife re-examination leads you to wholesome recreational activities, great! And hey, you could even spend your midlife crisis with a second honeymoon and fall in love with your spouse all over again!

It's only when it leads you away from your covenants or into debt or weirdness that we have a problem.

Threat Level: Quicksand

Overall, the midlife crisis is like quicksand. (Note: Some types of midlife crises carry different threat levels.) Quicksand may be found at various spots on the journey to happily ever after, but it doesn't have to be fatal. It really doesn't kill that many people, and it really doesn't have to kill you. It's not that hard to spot. It really doesn't suck you down that quickly. In fact, it's pretty slow. As long as you stay by your Guide, He can easily throw you a line to rescue you from it. Better still, He knows all the spots where it's found along the way, making it pretty simple to avoid. But for some reason, sticking with the Guide is a problem for a whole lot of people on this journey.

Q: How do I know if I'm having a midlife crisis?

A: Don't worry about that. Just worry about where it's taking you.

Honestly, a midlife crisis is a pretty naturally occurring thing. It happens all the time, and it does not have to be a bad thing. My running and my wife's return to school both might fit under the umbrella of a midlife crisis in some people's opinions, so a "midlife crisis" is not an insult at all. Don't worry about the title. Just worry about whether it takes you away from your covenants to any degree. If it over-emphasizes worldliness, leads you to debt, or compromises your commitment to the Lord, *then* you need to worry.

Q: What are some forms of a harmful midlife crisis?

A: Sowing wild oats is a big one. (Note: Higher threat level with this one.)

Some people—too many people—freak out in their midlife because they want to try new and sometimes extreme things. Many times those new things just aren't good. I've worked with many, many marriages in which someone said that he or she got married too young and didn't get to live it up before getting married. Now, when they want to experience this thrill, it leads them to alcohol, drugs, or partying. That never ends well. That obviously leads people away from their covenants.

People in this kind of crisis often say that they didn't get to date enough people, so they're going to try dating others now, while they're still married. No, that doesn't work at all. That most definitely leads people away from their covenants.

Some people in this kind of midlife crisis decide that maybe they're really gay, so they give that a try. That takes people away from their covenants and brings misery.

When people try these new things, even though wickedness never was happiness (Alma 41:10), they still may try to salvage some level of happiness or "freedom" from this experiment. That means they keep going down this path, or they experiment in other new paths, basically trying to find out how many wrongs *will* make a right, since the first two didn't do the trick.

Whatever the new paths might be, this kind of midlife crisis is characterized by wild experimentation and rebellion. The only cure for this is straightforward repentance, but this is usually the last thing that people having this kind of crisis want to hear. They want no rules or at least fewer rules, not some kind of code to follow. Many people in this kind of crisis stray so far from their covenants that they often end up leaving the Church altogether.

Threat Level: Cliffs

Cliffs are only dangerous if you get too close to them. Since cliffs don't move, the danger they pose is completely preventable. Some people get bored on the journey, so they want to venture off the map or run to a cool-looking place when they think the Guide isn't watching. That venture can take them right off a cliff to their own demise. Everybody knows the cliffs are there, so it's hard to believe that people still fall off them so regularly. But they do.

Some people want to live on the edge, but the Guide always wants to keep them far from the edge because He doesn't want them to fall off. Some people want to dance on the edge of a cliff, and they fall off.

Some people stray near a cliff because they're wandering in the darkness. They don't know where they're going because they just can't see. Before they know it, they've walked straight off the cliff because their eyes are closed, or they just don't walk in the light.

Some people even jump off the cliff on purpose, thinking it will be fun to jump into the water below. They run at the cliff with their eyes wide open, looking forward to the big cannonball in the ocean at the bottom of the cliff. But no. The water isn't deep enough to break their fall, and they hit it so hard that it might as well be concrete.

Q: What other kind of midlife
crisis should we be aware of?

A: The cumulative effect midlife crisis.

I think many times people get divorced in their forties or fifties
not so much because somebody is freaking out but because problems that have festered for years and years have finally come to
a head. With years of frustrations piled up, somebody just plain
loses it and cries uncle. I call this the cumulative effect midlife
crisis. It is a culmination of lots of other problems, including the
problems that get their own sections. They come together here.

Q: What are some of these cumulative effects?

A: In no particular order, let's start with
sexual differences. (Note: This one
has varying threat levels too.)

Let's make some generalizations and see this through the husband's and wife's eyes separately. Men tend to have stronger sex
drives than women. Let's say that a husband and wife got married in their early or mid-twenties and are now in their mid-for-
ties, when a midlife crisis typically hits. That's twenty plus years
of marriage. During those twenty plus years, let's assume that a
husband has tried to initiate sexual activity two or three times a
week. Because of the difference in drives, most of those attempts
have failed. Over those twenty-plus years, the husband's failed
attempts have just about added up to two or three thousand.

The husband sees this as twenty years of persistent rejection.
As he sees it, his lifetime strikeout total is now shameful, painful,
and probably even humiliating. If he were a major leaguer, he
would hold the all-time record for strikeouts as a hitter.

On the other hand, the wife sees this as twenty years of a guy who just doesn't get it. He has no idea what it's like taking care of children all day, trying to keep the house clean, juggling callings, driving children everywhere. She sees this one-track-minded guy trying to give her one more ball to juggle when that's the last thing she needs or wants. And the guy just won't stop! Does he see her as anything beyond a sex partner?

She might also see it as twenty years of built-up guilt. She feels terrible that she just doesn't have the same desires he has. She doesn't like the toll it has taken on her marriage. She feels like a failure for not making her husband happier. Every time he tries something, the guilt comes back, and few things kill a mood like guilt does.

More likely, it's a combination of these two situations. The guilt and the pestering have merged to the point where it's not worth wondering or trying to figure out which one is the bigger problem. Either way, enough is enough.

Their frustration spills over into just about every aspect of their marriage. The husband goes to work wondering what's wrong with him and wishing his wife were more like so-and-so's. That guy never gets turned down. He always comes to work with a smile on his face. The husband dreams of what it would be like to have a wife who loves him that much. His thoughts wander away from his wife. He avoids her. Disagreements come up much more easily. Either he takes out his frustrations in the way he treats her or he just withdraws.

The wife feels alone all day. Her needs to communicate about all their joint responsibilities go unfulfilled because her husband is withdrawn or short-tempered. She's afraid to let him touch her at all because she knows what will come next, and she's definitely not in the mood to have sex with a guy who doesn't brighten the room or treat her well.

And the cycle feeds itself again and again. Well, after twenty or so years of this, at least one of the spouses is tired of the tears and the cycle. One of them calls a lawyer and files for divorce. It's over.

The roles could easily be reversed. Wives can feel the same way as the husband in this example. That doesn't matter. What matters is that years of frustration take their toll, and that dooms the marriage.

Threat Level: Dehydration, Heat Stroke, and Exposure

Dehydration can indeed kill. Even when it doesn't kill, it takes its toll on every aspect of your functioning, including your stamina to make it through the day and your ability to think clearly. The quest for happily ever after is a very long and arduous journey. Be sure to take plenty of water and sunscreen on this journey to avoid this problem. Men tend to need more of it than women. And please, please be sure that the water you take on the journey comes from a pure source.

Q: What other cumulative effect crises are there?

A: Unkind words. (Note: This one has varying threat levels as well.)

In the example above, I used two or three thousand cumulative sexual advance rejections, as the husband saw it. That number seems a little staggering when it builds up over the years, doesn't it? Now take the total of unkind words exchanged by marital partners over the years. That number is probably far greater than the number of failed advances. It may easily be ten times greater. Can you imagine twenty or thirty thousand cumulative unkind words through the years? Yeah, that would hurt anybody. That would be enough to make all sorts of people call it quits.

Lawyers see texts and emails between divorcing spouses very regularly. The unkind words in these "communications" are atrocious and heartbreaking. You want to take a shower after reading them. You want to find a way to wash your eyes and ears out. These couples didn't hit that level of meanness overnight. They spent a long time mastering the art of hurtful words. Maybe if they had stopped earlier, they would not be working with a lawyer.

Q: Can you be a little more specific with what you mean by "unkind words"?

A: You know what I mean.

- If it chases away the Holy Ghost, it's unkind.
- If it hurts or insults, it's unkind.
- If it belittles, it's unkind.
- If it doesn't build, it's probably unkind or at least unnecessary.
- If it's an expletive, it's definitely unkind.
- If it's judgmental, it's unkind.
- If it's unfair, it's unkind.
- If you say it with a raised voice, it's probably unkind, no matter what word it actually is.
- If the word spoken is "dumb" or "stupid," it is definitely unkind. In fact, it borders on and may well be abuse. In my opinion, if you're uttering these words to or about your spouse, you are not worthy of a temple recommend on this ground alone.

President Gordon B. Hinckley taught, "Who can calculate the wounds inflicted, their depth and pain, by harsh and mean words spoken in anger? How pitiful a sight is a man who is strong in many ways but who loses all control of himself when some little thing, usually of no significant consequence, disturbs his equanimity. In every marriage there are, of course, occasional differences. But I find no justification for tempers that explode on the slightest provocation" ("Our Solemn Responsibilities," *Ensign,* November 1991).

The human heart can only take so much. Years of unkind words suck the life out of a spouse. You really can't blame him or her at this point for wanting out.

If you have any doubt where you rank on this subject, please try filling your marriage with kind words. So many women have told me over the years how ugly and unwanted they feel because so many unkind words have built up. Those women need to be told how wonderful, how beautiful—and every woman who reflects the light of Christ is beautiful in a very real way—and how important they are. Those words are priceless. Fill your spouse's ears with words of praise, and you will fill her heart with happiness.

> "All little girls should be told they're pretty."
>
> —Marilyn Monroe

Threat Level: Mosquito

Unkind words are without a doubt the mosquito on this journey. They seem tiny and annoying, like a petty annoyance. Why would you fear a little old mosquito on this journey? Because in reality the mosquito is the world's deadliest animal. And it's not even close. It kills around one million people a year and transfers diseases to approximately seventy million people each year. Those numbers are shocking, and that is what adds to the mosquito's threat. Like unkind words, mosquitoes usually attack in droves. People don't think of a mosquito as deadly, just as a pain. After all, hasn't everyone been bitten by a mosquito? Yes, and everyone occasionally utters unkind words. The mosquito does not kill by itself, like a venomous snake or a vicious carnivore; it kills by spreading all sorts of diseases. Unkind words inflict any number of diseases that permeate the marriage and kill it. Do not mess with the mosquito. It is more than just a pain; it kills like no other creature.

Q: How do you deal with this cumulative effect?

A: Stop it. Try to repent and change, and try to forgive.

Like any of these subjects, you need to approach in the attitude of "Lord, is it I?" (Matthew 26:22).

If you are guilty of any of these examples, stop it now. Repent now. For more information, see the section on mercy. Since both sides are probably guilty of this, both have to stop, and both have to seek mercy.

But please understand that it still may be too late. Many spouses are numb by this point. They come into the lawyer's office with blank stares or tears. Their esteem is destroyed. They are past feeling. They would love to see a change, but almost always, changes have been promised before, many, many times.

Those promises have not been delivered. It's hard to believe that this time will be any different.

Q: Any other cumulative effects crises to be aware of?

A: It can really be just about anything if it's carried on long enough.

Over enough time, even a steady drip of one water droplet at a time can cut and shape rock. It can certainly create stalagmites and stalactites. If any problem is persistent enough, it can become a cumulative effect crisis and can lead to a divorce. Some couples can tolerate it longer and reach their limit in their sixties or seventies. So a cumulative effect crisis is not just limited to people in or around their forties.

COVENANT DRIFT

I f I were to list the most ugly, contentious, and painful divorces I've been involved in or have seen over twenty years in this business, the majority of them would be LDS divorces. We're talking about the kind of divorce so gross and so militant that it takes months off the lawyer's life expectancy and, it's safe to assume, years off the parties' life expectancies.

Why? I can answer that question very simply: When a run-of-the-mill marriage goes bad, it's a social contract broken. When an LDS marriage goes bad, it's a covenant broken. When covenants are broken, we end up in someone else's power. That's not pretty. In fact, it's flat-out devastating. The consequences can be eternal.

Especially in marriage, our covenants are not just the lifeline to blessings from heaven, they are protection from storms and threats. The Savior is the only sure foundation on which we can build and the only foundation that can survive storms (Matthew 7:24–29; Helaman 5:12). Not only does He, our Guide, provide the only safe foundation, He, as the rock of our salvation, also provides shelter and safety from wars and forces who want to destroy us (1 Nephi 3:27; Ether 13:13–14). If you want to deepen your understanding of this, substitute *blessings* or *protection* any time you read the word the word *covenant*. Nobody wants to lose blessings, and we certainly can't afford to lose protection on this journey. Our covenants are the last thing we want to take lightly in life.

Q: What do you mean by "covenant drift"?

A: When couples stray from their baptismal and temple covenants, individually or collectively.

To be sure, most of the other threats discussed in this book represent some level of broken or neglected covenants. With this particular threat, I am speaking primarily—but certainly not exclusively—of spouses who drift from their covenants, sometimes together. When people drift from their covenants, they tend to drift apart from each other sooner or later. When they aren't true to their covenants, the Spirit withdraws from the home. Couples may hang in there a while if they drift together, but they do so at their own peril. By drifting from their covenants, they build a wall between themselves and the blessings promised through their covenants.

Usually, one person drifts further or faster than the other. When that drift is sudden or thick, that's when hate really steps in, and the battle gets fierce and disgusting. A couple may collectively decide that they no longer need or want their covenants. For example, every once in a while, some couples decide to experiment with pornography or other sexual adventures together, thinking it will spice up their lives. They're wrong. When they drift together, they will almost certainly end up drifting apart at some point.

"Stay on target! Stay on target!"

—Davish Krail, Y-Wing Fighter Pilot

As always, there are levels of covenant drift. Some are gradual, and many couples can hang in for a while. In others, Satan truly bares his fangs and makes a monster of one or both spouses.

Threat Level:
Boa Constrictor or Python

Huge snakes like this don't kill you with their venom and fangs; they kill you by crushing you. They don't sneak up on you like other serpents on this journey to happily ever after because they're big and fat, not particularly agile. You have to either be playing with them, get stupidly close to them, or fall asleep in a dangerous place for them to get ahold of you. But when they do get ahold of you, you are gone. You will be crushed. No matter how strong you are, you will not escape the deadly, crushing grip of these serpents. You are no longer in your own power; you're under the serpent's power.

Q: How can I tell if covenant drift is happening in my marriage?

A: It often starts with how you treat sacred things.

Like any of these subjects, both spouses need to be asking, "Lord, is it I?" Even when one spouse is clearly drifting and may be further from his or her covenants, the other spouse remains imperfect. Both can benefit from examining and re-examining where they stand before the Lord regularly.

Beyond that, the first noticeable signs of covenant drift show up in how people treat sacred things.

For example, have you slacked off paying tithing? This represents a lack of consecration when you don't view those funds as sacred, and you stop offering this sacrifice to the Lord.

Do you wear the temple garment day and night? If not, you are beginning to treat this sacred thing as less than sacred. This is a surprisingly big one because the garment represents and is a reminder of your covenants. When you stop treating it as sacred and instead treat it as worldly, you are experiencing covenant drift. You would be surprised at how often this one shows up.

Do you really, truly keep the Sabbath day holy? It is a sacred time, set apart from the cares of the world every week. When people find themselves spending the Sabbath away from sacred things, it is another telltale sign that they are drifting. The sacrament that we partake of on the Sabbath is intended to be a deep, introspective "Lord, is it I?" moment each and every week. We lose the benefit of that blessing if we are not keeping the Sabbath holy by attending our meetings and truly worshipping.

Then, of course, there is the temple. It is the most sacred of spaces. Is this sacred space a regular and indispensable part of your life?

Closely behind the temple in terms of sacredness is the home. When people don't fill the home with things that invite the Spirit, they are drifting. This happens with entertainment, internet, unkind words, and so on. You get the picture.

Some of these are harder to detect than others. My point is simply that covenant drift often begins with a lack of respect for sacred things. Of these, wearing the temple garment and activities on the Sabbath are surprisingly accurate indicators of covenant drift.

Q: How do I stop covenant drift?

A: Repent.

Repentance is the answer to a whole lot of questions, isn't it? This is why I believe mercy is the single most important gospel principle in marriage. This is also why you have to call out to your Guide to rescue you. If you truly want His help, He will give it. Nobody has to be crushed by this serpent.

SELF-RIGHTEOUSNESS

There are varying degrees of self-righteousness. At its lightest, it's annoying. At its worst, self-righteousness is flat-out oppressive in a marriage. It includes controlling behavior, inability to see the good in others, ingratitude, constant unkind words, and an unquestioned betrayal of covenants. Yet somehow, self-righteous spouses see nothing wrong with themselves. They think everything they do is fine—beautiful and holy, even—while their spouse simply can't keep up with them.

Male Threat Level:
The Emperor

This is not the Sith Lord from Star Wars; it's the one from Hans Christian Andersen—the vain, self-absorbed emperor who is under the false impression that he's beautifully arrayed in gorgeous robes, when he's actually wearing nothing. Obsessed with his title and his appearance at the expense of his character, he thinks he looks like a million bucks. This symbolism takes on a different level, since robes are sometimes used to symbolize the priesthood (for example, Joseph and the coat of many colors).

The emperor thinks he carries the priesthood, but in reality the Lord has said amen to the priesthood of the man who exercises unrighteous dominion (D&C 121:37).

Notice with both the male and female threat levels here that self-righteousness is not an outside threat. Instead, the self-righteous man or woman *becomes* the threat. That is the nature of self-righteousness. We don't even realize that we have become the villain. We remain convinced that we are the queen or the emperor, all caught up in our illusion of righteousness.

Q: What do you mean by "self-righteousness"?

A: In men, it mostly surfaces as unrighteous dominion. In women, it tends to be a toxic air of superiority.

This marital poison tends to manifest itself differently in men and women. In either case, it is a problem that very few people recognize they have.

Let's talk about the men's problems first. The Doctrine and Covenants teaches, "We have learned by sad experience that it is the nature and disposition of almost all men, as soon as they get a little authority, as they suppose, they will immediately begin to exercise unrighteous dominion. Hence, many are called, but few are chosen. No power or influence can or ought to be maintained by virtue of the priesthood, only by persuasion, by long-suffering, by gentleness and meekness, and by love unfeigned; By kindness, and pure knowledge, which shall greatly enlarge the soul without hypocrisy and without guile" (D&C 121:39–42).

Men tend to have big (yet at the same time remarkably fragile) egos. It seems like an oxymoron, but it's real. Men try to balance their fragile egos by asserting control. That's what we call unrighteous dominion. The Doctrine and Covenants teaches plainly, "it is the nature and disposition of almost all men" to take a little authority, like the authority of being a priesthood holder and a husband, and begin to abuse it. (D&C 121:39) The calling of husband or father tends to give LDS men a false air of righteousness, which they tend to feed with references to the priesthood. They believe that Adam was created before Eve, and Eve was told to follow her husband, because that's how the priesthood works. They think they're the best thing that ever happened to their spouses. But a man who truly honors the priesthood that he holds views his wife as the best thing that ever happened to him.

At the same time, many LDS women going through a divorce have shown themselves to be unbearably self-righteous. They can hardly pass up a chance to tell people how pure and excellent they are, while their husbands wallow in the mire like pigs. They've never made any mistakes. Except, of course, for marrying an inferior, incompetent loser. It's okay, though. They will probably be taken up to heaven like Elijah in a chariot as soon as the divorce is final and they are free from the spiritual deadweight that is their husbands.

Okay, I'm exaggerating, but you get the point.

Q: How does this show up in men?

A: If you ever find yourself saying something like . . .

"Because I'm the priesthood holder," then you're in trouble. If you expect your wife or your children to bow down to you because you are a man or because you hold the priesthood, you are woefully wrong. You need to read section 121 very carefully and very slowly, all the while asking yourself, "Lord, is it I?"

The Lord did not make you the first accountable person in your family because you can do no wrong. No, He appointed you as the primarily responsible person in your family based on the condition that you follow Him. If you are not acting in kindness, meekness, gentleness, and unfeigned love, then you are not leading at all; you are doing a disservice and setting a bad example that your children are painfully likely to follow when they grow up. If you act as the head of your family in any degree of unrighteousness, then "the heavens withdraw themselves; the Spirit of the Lord is grieved; and when it is withdrawn, Amen to the priesthood or authority of that man" (D&C 121:37). That means you are not acting in the priesthood at all if you are acting unrighteously. Your unrighteousness takes away your very claim to leadership.

If you find yourself "leading" your family by yelling, saying unkind things, coercing people, and not leading gently as the Savior would, then you are acting in unrighteous dominion.

Wake up! You do not know everything. I promise.

Q: But aren't men supposed to take the lead in the home?

A: Priesthood holders are to honor the priesthood as they preside in the home.

"The Family: A Proclamation to the World" lists three primary duties that husbands and fathers owe to their families: preside, provide, and protect. All three of these words begin with a prefix indicating "before" or "in front of." This means that your duties place you in front of the rest of the family, not because you're better but because you are the first one the Lord will hold accountable in the family. It means your family should be able to look up to you, not have you look down on them.

If you have taken any of these duties to mean that you are the "captain" of the ship, then there are a few things that you have to understand in the context of the duties the Lord has placed on you. First, understand that if you enjoy being the captain because you get to feel cool and tell other people what to do, then you are not much of a captain. Your goal should be to get your crew and cargo safely to their destination, not to stoke your own ego. Your crew and cargo are your family, and your destination is to return them to Heavenly Father. Nothing could be more precious to Him. Second, understand that, because you are responsible for the ship and everybody on it, you are the one who is held accountable if anything goes wrong. Third, understand that if your ship sinks, you go down with it. Those are the rules that captains follow.

Here is my point: The Lord has placed you as the primarily responsible party. He has given you a responsibility. With this gift and this charge, you are the one He looks to when it comes to getting His children under your care back to Him. This is purely a matter of responsibility.

In 1965, President David O. McKay made the following statement to a group of Church employees:

> Let me assure you, Brethren, that some day you will have a personal priesthood interview with the Savior himself. If you are interested, I will tell you the order in which he will ask you to account for your earthly responsibilities.
>
> First, he will request an accountability report about your relationship with your wife. Have you actively been engaged in making her happy and ensuring that her needs have been met as an individual?
>
> Second, he will want an accountability report about each of your children individually. He will not attempt to have this for simply a family stewardship but will request information about your relationship to each and every child.
>
> Third, he will want to know what you personally have done with the talents you were given in the preexistence.

Fourth, he will want a summary of your activity in your Church assignments. He will not be necessarily interested in what assignments you have had, for in his eyes the home teacher and a mission president are probably equals, but he will request a summary of how you have been of service to your fellow man in your Church assignments.

Fifth, he will have no interest in how you earned your living but if you were honest in all your dealings.

Sixth, he will ask for an accountability on what you have done to contribute in a positive manner to your community, state, country, and the world. (From the notes of Fred A. Baker, Managing Director, Department of Physical Facilities, quoted by Elder Robert D. Hales, "Understandings of the Heart," BYU Devotional, March 15, 1988)

Yes, men, you have many responsibilities. Above all of them—as important as it is to be a provider for your family's needs—is your need to be a good husband. Your need to be a good father is a very close second. Both of these duties are fulfilled in the home. If you are not a good husband, it is very difficult to be a good father, and vice versa. You absolutely cannot afford to fail in these duties. They are the lifeline of your eternity.

In fact, I am willing to bet that any truly successful mission president and his wife will tell you that their main goal in watching over hundreds of young men and women was not to baptize. I bet they will tell you that their first goal was to grow the Church by raising up strong, righteous future husbands and fathers, wives and mothers. I bet they will tell you that their secondary goal was to grow the Church by raising up future leaders for the Church. I bet they will tell you that their third goal was to grow the Church through convert baptisms. Once again, we see that the qualities and exhortations of section 4 of the Doctrine and Covenants apply to marriage and parenting equally as well as they apply to missionary work. And once again, we see that our top priority as men and priesthood holders should be to our wives and children.

Let me follow up these rather blunt words with a word of encouragement. The Lord put His trust in you. That means you have the ability to lead in righteousness and the ability to change when needed. You have the ability to bless your family like no one else. You can't do it in unrighteous dominion, but you can do it if you will repent. Please, for the sake of your family and your bride, wake up, repent, and change when needed.

Now that we've spoken plainly to the men, on to the sisters.

Female Threat Level: The Evil Queen

She thinks she is the fairest of them all. She wants to be recognized and known as the fairest of them all. In reality, she is an evil witch. But still, she's the queen. Just ask her.

Q: How does this problem reveal itself in women?

A: You don't even have to ask her. She will tell you how good she is or how bad her husband is. Probably both.

For as seriously as I take unrighteous dominion—because I believe the Lord certainly expects more from those who hold His priesthood—I have actually encountered many more self-righteous women in my career. It has been shocking to me. (And it sure has made me grateful for my own wife!)

These women are easy to spot in court. Nothing has ever been their fault. After five or ten questions that they respond to by insulting their husbands and extolling themselves, I can summarize their positions by asking them, "So, everything you do is right, and everything he does is wrong?" And you won't believe their answer. "Yes." If the wife is that brazen in front of a judge who will decide her fate, you can only imagine how she has been in the home.

You could call this henpecking, if you're familiar with that term.

You could also call this nagging.

Earlier, you read my observation that Satan is going after the wives and mothers in Zion right now with everything he has. I believe feeding a woman's sense of self-righteousness is one of his strongest tactics in attacking women and tearing down the family. If you think about it, this follows his pattern. He takes things with a kernel of truth—such as the divinity of women and their irreplaceable role in nurturing the family—and then twists it. He makes them think they're infallible, not just invaluable. Of course, he follows the same pattern with men. His current playbook just seems to emphasize it more with women.

Husbands of these women come into the lawyer's office just spent. They have no confidence. They feel like doormats, being walked on constantly. They can't say anything without being told how inferior they are or at least hearing how good their wives are. Sometimes they can barely look you in the eye. They have been trying to hit a moving target of what their wives expect from them, but the target never seems to stop moving. Nothing they do is good enough to keep up with their perfect wives, who are quick to remind them of it.

These are also the wives who are most likely to use children as pawns and treat them like property instead of people. They turn children against the other parent. To me, that is abominable.

These women are lulled to sleep by their own misguided belief that they are innocent or at least justified and that everything is really their husbands' fault.

Self-righteous spouses, whether they are male or female, are about as flexible as granite. Try to bend it, and it will shatter. These spouses are far past the ability to see any redeeming good in each other. These spouses fill each other's ears with unkind words each day.

Pardon my bluntness on this subject. I am trying to be an equal-opportunity offender for both men and women because people sometimes need to be offended if they are going to change. Remember, the most deadly snakes don't make noise to warn you before they strike and kill you. Let this be that noise that startles you out of harm's way.

And now, speaking to both men and women . . .

Q: What can be done about it?

A: Self-righteousness is about feeling superior. Humility is the cure.

When I was little, my mother taught me that people insult other people because they want to feel superior. They can do that either by building themselves up or by cutting others down. That is exactly how self-righteousness works. Spouses want to build themselves up, and they do that by cutting others down. Except that doesn't make them any better, does it? It just makes them bullies.

President Thomas S. Monson taught a beautiful lesson on self-righteousness, pointing out those who believe themselves to be so divine and superior are often not what they believe.

From ancient times comes an example which emphasizes this truth. Darius, through the proper rites, had been recognized as legitimate king of Egypt. His rival, Alexander, had been declared legitimate son of Ammon; he, too, was Pharaoh. Alexander found the defeated Darius on the point of death and laid his hands upon his head to heal him, commanding him to arise and resume his kingly power, concluding, "I swear unto thee, Darius, by all the gods, that I do these things truly and without fakery," to which Darius replied with a gentle rebuke, "Alexander, my boy . . . do you think you can touch heaven with those hands of yours?" (Thomas S. Monson, "That We May Touch Heaven," *Ensign,* November 1990)

Brothers and sisters, if you truly believe your hands are in contact with heaven, but your marriage is a wreck, please take a good look at those hands. The contaminants on your hands may not be visible to you, like a camouflaged snake blending in with its surroundings, but they are most assuredly there, and they are toxic to your marriage. The true condition of your hands can only be seen with a healthy dose of humility, a sincere "Lord, is it I?"

But your hands can be washed! Your Guide has the power to wash them. He has the power to extend their reach to heaven. It will take a lot of work. Most of all, it will require you to open your eyes to see the impurities on your hands. If you don't see them, you won't even know how they are killing your marriage.

Q: Can you leave us with some less depressing advice on this subject?

A: Sure. Watch for extremes.

As part of their everything-he-or-she-does-is-wrong-and-everything-I-do-is-right mentality, spouses in this trap of self-righteousness tend to deal in absolutes. But some of these absolutes are easier to catch before you hit full-on attack-and-hate mode. For example, if you find yourself saying "always" or "never" in a negative way about your spouse, that's when you can and should stop yourself. "We always do what you want." "You never listen to me." It may seem to you that everything is so extreme, so black and white, but it almost certainly isn't. I won't go as far as to say that only a Sith deals in absolutes, but you can and should stop if you find yourself using these extreme words about your spouse.

Look, marriage is not like an old western movie or TV show. There isn't a clear-cut bad guy and a clear-cut Roy Rogers or the Lone Ranger. Both people have some good and some less-than-good qualities. When you find yourself thinking or speaking in absolutes or extremes, that is the time to stop before you're standing on top of the deadly camouflaged snake.

Sexual Issues

Once again, I rely on the words of the prophet, seer, and revelator Spencer W. Kimball. "If you study the divorces, as we have had to do in these past years, you will find there are one, two, three, four reasons. Generally, sex is the first. They did not get along sexually. They may not say that in the court. They may not even tell that to their attorneys, but that is the reason" (*The Teachings of Spencer W. Kimball* [Salt Lake City: Bookcraft, 1982], 312–314).

Why are sexual issues such a problem? Consider also the words of President David O. McKay.

> In my experience there is another reason [for divorce] that seems not so obvious but that precedes and laces through all of the others. It is the lack of constant enrichment in marriage. It is an absence of that 'something extra' which makes married life precious, special, and wonderful, in spite of its being sometimes drudgery, difficult, and dull. ("Experiencing Happiness in Marriage," *Teachings of Presidents of the Church: David O. McKay,* 2011)

Let's focus on this "constant enrichment" comment from President McKay for a bit, shall we? He didn't specifically mention sex, but I think it applies. I already made a bold promise that regular, worthy temple attendance will bless your marriage like nothing else. Clearly, temple attendance is something that "enriches" marriage in spades. I also stated that reading scriptures and praying together each day provides a constant enrichment to your marriage. What else?

Well, let's consider the first scripture on the subject of marriage: the instructions given to Adam and Eve and to us as their children. "Therefore *shall* a man leave his father and his mother, and *shall* cleave unto his wife: and they *shall* be one flesh" (Genesis 2:24; emphasis added). The verb *shall* is the same verb that accompanies the Ten Commandments. There are some challenges in the Hebrew-to-English translation process, but this instruction to leave father and mother, to cleave (to adhere closely, to cling), and to be one flesh appears to be an actual commandment. Consider also the punctuation of the scripture in English. The first two instructions are followed by a colon, suggesting that they lead up to the final instruction of being one flesh. Understanding this scripture, can there be any question that sexual relations are divinely appointed, even commanded within marriage?

I submit that sexual relations, as a divinely appointed part of marriage, are "something extra" that can or should enrich your marriage. This part of marriage is certainly "something extra" that "makes married life precious, special, and wonderful, in spite of its being sometimes drudgery, difficult, and dull" (McKay, "Experiencing Happiness in Marriage"). That's a significant part of the enrichment that we need to keep marriages from failing!

Sexual relations are indeed divinely appointed—even commanded—in marriage. The challenge is to align the husband and wife as closely as possible so that sex serves as a blessing to the marriage and not a curse.

Threat Level: Dehydration, Possible Waterborne Diseases

I've mentioned this threat before when I talked about different kinds of cumulative effect midlife crises. Remember that everybody needs water to survive. Frankly, sex plays a similar role in a marriage's survival. When water gets sparse on this long journey to happily ever after, some spouses go looking for anything they can find to quench their thirst. Many times this leads them to contaminated water where waterborne diseases thrive. Real-world diseases from contaminated water sources kill a staggering 3.4 million people per year around the globe. Many times the waterborne disease is not fatal by itself, but it weakens the body's immune system so much that it falls prey to another ailment. Sexual differences work the same way. When the bonding, affection, harmony, and love of a healthy sexual relationship are replaced with frustration, loneliness, and discord caused by sexual differences, then other problems creep in. If the problems have already crept in, they are harder to defend and recover from in the absence of a strong sexual relationship.

Q: What can be done about this?

A: Great news! This is very treatable!

I am not an expert on this subject. Lawyers hear the occasional frustrated comment from their clients about this subject. Beyond that, President Kimball is right—it's not something that is mentioned in a courtroom.

What I can definitely say about this subject is this:

1. Women find few things as unsexy as laziness. Husbands, if you are not absolute pros at laundry, dishes, vacuuming,

and so forth, and if you're not doing at least one of them on a daily basis, then you are missing out. If you instead are an expert on TV shows and sports broadcasts, then you can definitely do something to help yourself be a little more appealing to your wife.

2. Flames will burn out if the fire is not kept going. There is a reason why the Topical Guide in your scriptures has a whole section on continuing courtship in marriage. Plan a date night regularly, and keep it. Be the very best kind of multitasker and include temple worship in your dates.

3. Be kind. Please be kind. Remember, unkind words are like mosquitoes, and they kill more people than any other creature in the world.

4. Get your water from a pure source. Sexual relations are beautiful and holy when kept inside a loving marriage. They are not something to be cheapened or exhibited for others. Keep the source of this water clean and pure. Do not introduce pornography of any level into the picture, thinking that it will spice things up and rev your engine. I've seen plenty of marital problems arise from this. Without question, there is good value in sex education because this is a very important part of marriage. It is so worth getting right. There are a number of good books available to help you that recognize and honor the sanctity of marital sexual relations. You can walk the line between education and smut without chasing the Spirit out of your marriage. Keep the fountain of this water pure.

5. Finally, don't overlook the sheer magic of a genuine, heartfelt, long, slow, tender kiss. It's a wonderful thing.

"Close your eyes, and I'll kiss you."

—The Beatles

Having said that, let me share some very good news with you from an actual expert on the subject.

> The success rate for psychotherapy [don't be put off by the word—just think of "counseling"] for sexual dysfunctions [don't be put off by this word, either—just think of "problems"] is actually quite high—higher, in fact, than most of the other problems I work with, such as depression and anxiety. Most sexual problems show significant improvement with therapy. (Thomas Holmans, *I Do. I Did? Now What?* 222)

How's that for good news? Professional intervention is very, very likely to offer you some real help on this subject! Your marriage doesn't need to die of dehydration or waterborne disease.

Let me finish the quote I started above:

Disorders often seen by counselors include disorders of the desire phase, which involves a lack of interest in sex or an active aversion to sex. These disorders may result from physical problems or illnesses that affect the balance of hormones in the body. Psychological factors can also play a role. Extreme avoidance, due to a fear of and an aversion to sex, is more likely among those who have been sexually abused.

Disorders of the arousal phase include erectile disorder, a male's inability to attain or maintain an erection, which has sometimes been called "impotence"; and female sexual arousal disorder, which describes a lack of lubrication of the vagina and a lack of other physical signs of sexual arousal, which has sometimes been called "frigidity." Those old terms have a negative connotation, and I prefer the newer names, although they sound very clinical.

Disorders of the orgasm phase include inhibited female orgasm, in which the woman rarely or never experiences orgasm; and inhibited male orgasm, a similar disorder in the male. While the disorders I've mentioned so far have a counterpart in both males and females, premature ejaculation, ejaculation before the man or his partner would like, is a disorder unique to males.

The problems I see most often are premature ejaculation in men and inhibited female orgasm in women. A key element in treating all types of sexual dysfunction is helping the couple decrease the anxiety and pressure to perform which are often associated with sex. In addition, there are specific exercises, depending on the nature of the disorder, which can be assigned to the couple as well.

If a couple wishes to pursue therapy, I recommend that they find a therapist who is reputable and licensed and has similar values to them. (Thomas Holmans, *I Do. I Did? Now What?* 222–23)

Q: Seriously, that's all you're going to say about sex?

A: No, I'm not done yet.

I just gave you the real good news and the most helpful advice up front. Counseling tends to be very successful in treating the problem! Now we're going to talk a little more specifically about the role that sexual relations play in the plan of salvation. You might not normally associate the plan of salvation with sexual relations too deeply, and that is something we need to change.

Looking back at the "cumulative effect midlife crisis" discussion, and then again at President Kimball's comments, there should be no question that differences in spouses' sex drives are a major problem. In the LDS Church, our culture can sometimes inadvertently add to that problem. We want so badly to teach our children the law of chastity that we often give the impression that sex is dirty, bad, gross, or at very least something that we shouldn't talk about. With that mindset, people, especially girls, enter marriage with an unhealthy attitude about sex. Laura Brotherson, who wrote the excellent and highly recommend book, *And They Were Not Ashamed—Strengthening Marriage through Sexual Fulfillment*, calls this "good girl syndrome."

There are two big problems with "good girl syndrome."

First, it's doctrinally incorrect. Our Father in Heaven did *not* create or ordain sexual relations as something evil. That is a dangerous and complete misreading of the plan of salvation. "Husband and wife . . . are authorized, in fact they are *commanded*, to have proper sex when they are married for time and eternity" (*The Teachings of Spencer W. Kimball* [Salt Lake City: Bookcraft, 1982], 312; emphasis added). "Good girl syndrome" is the result of misunderstood doctrine. Misunderstood doctrine is never good.

Second, "good girl syndrome" causes problems in marriage. This should be obvious from President Kimball's statements and the rest of this book. Read on, or reread the section on cumulative effect midlife crises.

Putting these two problems of "good girl syndrome" together, you can see how sexual differences are like waterborne diseases. If doctrine is like water in that it gives life, then incorrect doctrine is like contaminated water. Contaminated water gives rise to waterborne disease, which sends ripples throughout a marriage.

There is something we can and should do about this: We need to understand the correct doctrine and teach it to our children. That doctrine, correctly understood, will do more to change behavior on this subject than any other lecture I can give. Not only will a correct understanding of the doctrine prevent "good girl syndrome," it will also help us live the law of chastity much better.

Properly understood, sex is about aligning a husband and wife, bringing them as physically and spiritually close as humanly possible. Literally. It is about joining them and making them one. That is a beautiful and wonderful thing if you truly ponder it. I think of 3 Nephi 19. The Savior had been with the Nephites for a while. He had taught them pure doctrine. He had healed the sick among them. They had seen Him and touched Him. He had shown them miracles beyond words. He blessed their children in particular. The Holy Ghost was poured out on the people like never before. I can't even imagine how incredible this experience must have been. Even after this unforgettable experience, the level of spirituality was somehow still increasing, even when you think things were as perfect as possible. And in the midst of those great experiences, the Savior prayed.

What did He pray for in such an unimaginable display of glory and pure love? In a word, unity. "And now Father, I pray unto thee for them, and also for all those who shall believe on their words, that they may believe in me, that I may be in them as thou, Father art in me, that we may be one" (3 Nephi 19:23).

From this, I am led to believe that the concept of unity is among the most sacred and holy principles in eternity. That only makes sense since the English word *atonement* literally means to make "at one." I think we barely understand the sanctity of a husband and wife becoming one through sexual relations.

That level of bonding—of complete physical unity between a husband and wife—just can't be expected to flourish in the absence of unity throughout the rest of the marriage.

The "good girl syndrome" problems, any medical or clinical sexual problems, and the cumulative effect midlife crisis scenarios do not and cannot account for every case of sexual frustration in marriage. They account for a great many of the problems but certainly not all of them. To close the circle on this subject, I think you have to ask yourself constantly what could be done to improve your levels of unity throughout every other aspect of the marriage. If selfishness is permeating your marriage, then it's you *against* your spouse, not you *with* your spouse. That's anything but unity. If unkind words are anywhere in the marriage, that definitely kills unity. If one of you is in a spiritual rut and drifting from your covenants, that also tears you apart. If pornography is in the picture, then you're mentally engaging in some form of sex with someone who is not your spouse. That's a huge lack of unity. And so on and so on. I could go through everything in this book and the same conclusion would follow: If it's not building unity in the marriage itself, then it's hard to expect a healthy level of unity on the sexual front.

Earlier I mentioned that lawyers only get a few comments from clients on this subject. Those comments are borne out of frustration. Clients love to express their frustrations to their lawyers, but we don't delve deeper into the subject because it's just not legally relevant. Still, those comments about sex, taken with the rest of the failed marriage picture that we see, clearly show a complete lack of unity in the marriage. Is it any wonder there was no physical unity when there was such a lack of unity in so many other respects in the marriage? Maybe, just maybe, if they had worked on removing the divisiveness in the rest of their marriage, then the divisiveness on the sexual front would have lessened.

Wherever you start in the process of improving unity, just don't think that priming the pump on one end will automatically improve the other end. There still has to be an effort to improve unity at every point in the circle. As long as you're feeding the goal of unity, it should be a win–win situation, no matter where you start. Do as the Savior did in 3 Nephi 19. Pray specifically for unity.

PORNOGRAPHY

For years, the two most common themes I saw in divorces were debt and pornography. I am going to tackle pornography, but not by inflicting guilt or even by giving a self-help program outline. Pornography gets quite a bit of attention, to the point where those who struggle with it are probably sick of hearing about it and may tune it out altogether when it is brought up. I want to give you a different message. As for recovery from this problem, the Church has an outstanding addiction recovery program.

> *"If I get married,*
> *I want to be very married."*
>
> —Audrey Hepburn

Note: This lesson also applies to sexual differences in marriage and to our children. In fact, it is specifically written in a way that can be presented to youth.

Threat Level: Medusa

You've heard about Medusa. She's the lady whose hair is full of snakes. If you look at her, you turn to stone. She's deadly, but *only* if you look at her. She's out there all over the path to happily ever after. Rest assured, she will come looking for you. She might even try to carry on a conversation with you along the way. Just don't look at her, because, just like pornography, that's how she ruins you.

Sacred Things in Sacred Spaces

We normally associate the word *profanity* with foul language and taking the Lord's name in vain, and rightly so. But the word actually means much more than that. Broken down into its Latin roots, the word means "outside of" or "before" the temple. The temple is obviously a sacred space and a home for sacred things. When those sacred things are taken out of their sacred space, they are literally "outside of" or "before" the temple. They are literally profanity.

For example, the name of the Lord is something so sacred that it is to be spoken only in a sacred environment. Anciently, those surroundings were the innermost part of the temple itself. To honor the sanctity of the name of the Lord, the ancient Jews only uttered this sacred name one time per year—in the most sacred place (the Holy of Holies in the tabernacle or temple) on the most sacred day of the year (Yom Kippur, the Day of Atonement) by one consecrated person (the high priest, who actually represented the Savior Himself atoning for the sins of Israel). If that sacred name was ever spoken outside of its designated sacred space and sacred conditions, it was, by definition, profanity.

Obviously, today's world doesn't show this same respect for sacred things, especially the name of the Lord. His name now gets routinely dragged out of sacred space—the holy temple—and is paraded around with casualness and even anger. This is closer to the meaning of profanity that we're more familiar with, but it is not so much the bad language that is a lesson to us; it is taking something sacred out of its sacred space and protection.

Let's expand the examples of profanity a bit beyond words. We know the temple is sacred. For the most part, we are very good at respecting and maintaining the sacred ordinances of the temple. Yes, I think we're pretty good at this. But there are a few people who have sought to publish accounts or even pictures of sacred temple ordinances for the unworthy world to see. They have taken the sacred temple experience outside of its sacred space. That is profanity so gross that it makes my skin crawl, but these examples are relatively rare.

Now, as part of the sacred temple experience, it is no secret that people attending the temple wear sacred and special clothing. Can you imagine if someone took that sacred clothing and wore it around the home, to work, or to the store? Of course you can't. It sounds so wrong that you can't even think of it.

Here's another example—the sacrament is a weekly sacred ordinance that is administered in dedicated chapels. If we were at a basketball game, the last thing we would expect would be for someone to start screaming the sacrament prayer out loud. It's completely out of place, isn't it? Almost unimaginably so. Why? Well, we know full well that the sacrament is a sacred ordinance that is performed in a chapel by holders of the priesthood and under the direction of the bishop. That's where it belongs.

Let me give an example of something that is sacred on a personal level. A few years ago, I had the honor of appearing before the Supreme Court of the United States. Along with my wife and parents, I traveled to Washington DC for the event, and we got to tour some of the Smithsonian Museums. My wife and I thought it was super cool to see costumes from the original Harry Potter movie and even cooler to see one of the sunstones from the original Nauvoo Temple. But when we turned the corner in one museum, we were floored. There, in all her glory, was the original Star-Spangled Banner, the flag from Fort McHenry that inspired Francis Scott Key's national anthem. We were absolutely blown away. I would call that the single most awe-inspiring sight my eyes have ever beheld. The room was filled with a very real and a very palpable reverence. I hold that flag, like all the flags that have followed it, as sacred and dear. This emblem of the "heav'n rescued land," this monument to the "power that have made and preserved us a nation," is holy to me. ("The Star Spangled Banner," verse four) I am so grateful that the Smithsonian built and maintains a sacred space for this sacred emblem of our country. Without that sacred space, this flag would no doubt have been destroyed over the years. Because it is preserved in this protected place, it remains an awe-inspiring blessing for many.

Sacred things must be kept within their sacred spaces and their sacred atmosphere. The act of taking these sacred things out of their designated sacred spaces is literally profanity.

What are the sacred spaces for each of these?

For the ordinances and clothing of the temple, it is the temple.

For the sacrament, it is a dedicated chapel.

For the Star-Spangled Banner from Fort McHenry, it is the Smithsonian Museum.

Notice also that for the examples of the temple and the sacrament, these sacred ordinances require not just sacred places to

maintain their sanctity, but they also require a priesthood authority to oversee their administration. It is not just sacred spaces but
sacred authority that protects these sacred things.

The Sacred Space for Sexual Relations

Much like the name of the Lord in the temple in ancient Israel,
the Lord has dedicated a sacred space for sexual relations. That
sacred space is marriage. "The sacred powers of procreation are to
be employed only between man and woman, lawfully wedded as
husband and wife" ("The Family: A Proclamation to the World,"
Ensign, Nov. 2010, 129). Sexual relations between husband and
wife are a sacred thing ordained of God and a central part of the
plan of salvation. For that reason, they have been given a designated, dedicated sacred space. Taking them out of that sacred
space is profanity.

How exactly are sexual relations sacred? You remember our
words in the sexual issues chapter above about unity. I encourage
you to read that again.

Now add to that the words of Elder Jeffrey R. Holland.
When he was president of Brigham Young University, Elder
Holland taught of the sanctity of marital relations in a landmark address titled "Of Souls, Symbols, and Sacraments." In
this address, Elder Holland pointed out that sexual relations
are a union of our very souls, that they are symbols of a divine
union, and that they are a sacrament as a token of the power of
creation, which we share with our Father in Heaven. Yes, an act
that is in fact a union of souls, a symbol for divine unity, and
a form of a sacrament all in one is certainly something sacred.

Like the name of God in the ancient Holy of Holies, sexual relations are sacred and even worshipful when they are kept within the boundaries set by the Lord. To preserve their sanctity, they must be kept within their sacred space, which is marriage between one man and one woman. The act of taking them outside of that sacred space is a very grievous sin.

Like the temple and sacrament examples used above, the sacred space for sexual relations also involves a priesthood authority, namely a priesthood holder, acting in the place of the Savior, to "join" or "seal" a husband and wife together. In teaching the doctrine of marriage between a man and a woman, the Savior taught, "What therefore God hath joined together, let not man put asunder" (Matthew 19:6). How does God join a man and wife together? Through the sealing ordinance. That ordinance is conducted through the authority of the priesthood. Husband and wife enter the sacred space of marriage through the sacred power of the priesthood.

Within that sacred space—but only within that sacred space—sexual relations are not only good and proper, but they are actually *sacred*.

Q: So, what exactly do we need to teach our children about this?

A: We should have already taught them how to treat sacred things. Now teach them that sexual relations are sacred.

Kept within their proper space, sexual relations are not gross, awkward, or forbidden. They are not a subject we should change because we "just don't talk about that." That is doctrinally incorrect. Between husband and wife, sex is no more inappropriate than attending the temple or partaking of the sacrament. We may mean well to teach our children to keep the law of chastity by making the topic of sex awkward or forbidden. But it is doctrinally wrong.

And for remaining chaste—wouldn't our children be more likely to grow up chaste if they were taught to revere sexual relations and not fear them? In my experience, children are curious about sacred things, but they are not likely to push the limits on them. They are not likely to become overly obsessed with sacred things, and they are not likely to be overly curious about sacred things. I mean, have you ever heard of someone trying to break into the temple out of curiosity? Or have you ever heard of a child praying too much? No, a child's behavior is by nature not mischievous when it comes to things that the child understands as sacred.

The Lord taught Adam and Eve the plan of salvation by first teaching them the principles that underlie the laws (Alma 12:32). As we struggle to teach ourselves and our youth the importance of the law of chastity in today's society, perhaps the first step is to understand the principle behind the law.

If the topic of sex is difficult for you as a parent, let me suggest one other simple, straightforward way to teach it—a way designed for young children to understand it, even.

Here it goes:

The law of chastity is based on the principle—that means the truth and the understanding—that your body is a temple. That is the reason we don't do bad things to our body, like drink alcohol or smoke or take drugs. Because our bodies are a temple, and temples are sacred, certain parts of our body must be kept sacred. These are our private parts. We keep them sacred by not touching or playing with them, by not touching other people's private parts, and by not letting other people touch our private parts. It also means that we don't show these private parts off to other people, and we don't look at pictures or videos of people who do this. This is why we wear bathing suits and clothes that cover all of our private parts. This is because they are sacred, like the temple.

Simple as that.

Q: How exactly does this intersect with pornography?

A: Let's look at our "profanity" examples again.

To bring this point home, let's combine two of the examples of profanity we have discussed so far: the temple and the sacrament. The imagery of the restored temple is even more sacred to us than the sacrament. If the imagery of the temple (the pictures/clothing in our earlier examples) were taken so far out of its place that it became the subject of broadcasting at something like a basketball game, we would all be deeply offended. We would all be moved to do something about it to protect what we hold sacred. We would call the network to complain. We would boycott the network.

But do we realize that we permit the imagery of something similarly sacred, namely sexual relations, in our lives and even in our very homes on perhaps a daily basis? It comes through movies, music, the internet, and TV. It is, in a very real sense, the profane parading of something that God intended to be sacred. In that sense, pornography is much more like the basketball example, where someone starts shouting out the sacrament prayer at a basketball game, than society has trained us ever to realize.

This display of imagery of what was originally sacred is not just pornography; it is profanity. It is casting very sacred pearls before very foul swine. We cannot tolerate or entertain the parading of something as sacred as sexual relations outside of their proper bounds. Sacred things must be kept in their sacred spaces.

Q: How does pornography hurt a marriage?

A: The effect of taking sacred things out of their sacred spaces is a gradual but painful descent away from our covenants and away from the Holy Ghost.

Several years ago, Elder M. Russell Ballard came to Arizona for a regional conference. He spoke of pornography. What struck me most of his comments on the subject was a simple but unmistakable charge he gave to those of us present at that conference. "If any of you within the sound of my voice are involved in this, by apostolic charge, I say unto you to repent. It will desensitize you to the Spirit."

Now, it was very powerful to hear an Apostle give us a direct charge to run from this evil like the plague. But Elder Ballard's statement about the consequences of pornography ("It will desensitize you to the Spirit") did not seem like an incredibly strong warning at that time. I thought there were harsher things he could have said that still would have been true. Then, as time passed, I pondered the concept of being desensitized to the Spirit more.

The Holy Ghost taught me some lessons that impressed just how serious this consequence really is. The promised blessings of Doctrine and Covenants section 121 rang more deeply to me. Consider the great blessings that flow in large part from letting virtue garnish our thoughts unceasingly. "Then shall thy confidence wax strong in the presence of God; and the doctrine of the priesthood shall distil upon thy soul as the dews from heaven.

The Holy Ghost shall be thy constant companion, and thy scepter an unchanging scepter of righteousness and truth; and thy dominion shall be an everlasting dominion, and without compulsory means it shall flow unto thee forever and ever" (D&C 121:45–46).

This scripture alone teaches beautifully that virtuous thoughts—the direct opposite of pornography—are essential to having the Holy Ghost as our constant companion. That certainly is a good start to impressing the truth and importance of Elder Ballard's admonition.

When this scripture is contrasted with another moving scripture on the subject, Elder Ballard's admonition becomes even more meaningful. "And verily I say unto you, as I have said before, he that looketh on a woman to lust after her, or if any shall commit adultery in their hearts, they shall not have the Spirit"—so much for having the Holy Ghost as our constant companion—"but shall deny the faith"—so much for having the doctrine of the priesthood distill upon our souls like the dews from heaven—"and shall fear"—so much for our confidence waxing strong in the presence of God. (D&C 63:16)

The Book of Mormon takes this concept further. As I see it, a "hard heart" is closely aligned with being desensitized to the Spirit. What begins as a lack of sensitivity to the Spirit soon becomes a hardened heart. In one form or another, there are thirty-six references in the scriptures of having a hard heart. In 1 Nephi 2:18, the term is used to describe Laman and Lemuel, who are famous for their rebellion and failures. Then again in 2 Nephi 1:17, the term is again used to describe Laman and Lemuel and their descendants.

It appears in the scriptures that the next stage after having a hard heart is being "past feeling." Nephi uses this term in 1 Nephi 17:45 to describe Laman and Lemuel, who just a few chapters earlier *only* had hard hearts. Mormon uses the term "past feeling" in Moroni 9:20 to describe a Nephite civilization so lost and depraved that it literally killed itself off in war.

So, being "desensitized to the Spirit" does indeed look pretty tragic in light of the pattern taught in the Book of Mormon. There was a great deal of wisdom in Elder Ballard's apostolic charge to us, and there is a great deal of wisdom in keeping ourselves worthy of the constant companionship of the Holy Ghost, especially in marriage. Letting virtue garnish our thoughts unceasingly is an essential step in receiving those blessings.

The transition from being desensitized to the Spirit to hardening your heart to being past feeling describes all too perfectly what happens when pornography invades a marriage. At first, you go a little numb, not just to spiritual things but the needs of your wife and family. Unkind words come out too easily. Your wife may wonder, "What is wrong with me?"

Before long, your heart is hardened. Something else is taking over. The Holy Ghost is leaving your home. Your wife's feelings mean less and less to you. You tune them out as you go deeper and deeper. Before too long, you tune out other things she says. You wish she would just be quiet. You lose track of the good she does. Your covenants are becoming an afterthought, one that you are trying to tune out just like your wife's nagging, as you hear it.

Soon, she becomes your enemy. Your agency is pretty much a memory by now because you are hooked. By now, you are past feeling. You just want out.

We don't want to end up there, do we?

And to think all of this started by taking something sacred outside of its sacred space and sacred atmosphere. Put it back in its sacred place. Don't look at Medusa. Strengthen your foundation so that the Big Bad Wolf can't blow your house down. I promise—if you treat sexual relations as something sacred, you will welcome and revere the law of chastity.

Q: Any specific ideas about how we can protect against this?

A: Here are a few helpful ideas, but please get help if this problem has a hold on you.

Especially with a sin that preys on someone's agency like pornography, it is easier to avoid it in the first place than to repent of it later. Try putting a picture of the Savior on your computer screen. A wallet-sized picture the size of a pass-along card can fit easily in the corner of a computer monitor. A statue of the Savior or another picture of Him will fit neatly by the family television. You can't see the Savior out of the corner of your eye and continue with this other stuff.

In my opinion, no family computer should be without an internet filter. These are common and may even be built into the internet browser program already on the computer. At the same time, popular search engines have filter settings that also provide some level of protection.

And please don't be ashamed to see your bishop over this problem. It requires the keys of the gospel of repentance to clean up this problem. I promise you that your bishop will not look down on you for this. He will love you like a brother and will rejoice with you as you bury this problem. He may refer you to the Church's addiction recovery program. This is a truly inspired program that will help you immensely. He may give you a priesthood blessing to help you. He may have all sorts of insights to help you.

You need his help because this particular kind of problem needs to be cleaned in a special way. It needs to be buried. The

Book of Mormon teaches of a people converted to the Lord who were truly committed to abandoning their former sins. When these people were converted, they sought to "hide away" the swords that represented their former way of life before their conversion (Alma 24:15). In fact, these people buried their swords deep in the earth as a testimony and as a protection (Alma 24:16). As part of keeping their swords buried, they stayed very busy, laboring "abundantly with their hands" (Alma 24:18). Because these swords were buried away, these wonderful people gave their lives as a testament to their conversion and repentance (Alma 24:17–23).

Sexual sins are much like the people of Ammon's swords: They need be buried. You can't just drop them. If they are left around the house or on the ground, they are too easy to pick up again. They can cut us just by walking by them.

In burying these sins, be like the people of Ammon by staying busy (Alma 24:18). This kind of temptation runs rampant during a person's spare time, in moments of boredom and inactivity. In fact, my experience would lead me to call pornography an escape for people, more than anything else. If you are anxiously engaged and constantly filling your minds with truth, your lives with service, and your hearts with love, as President Monson has counseled us, you will literally not have the time to sin ("Be Thou an Example," *Ensign*, November 2001). Bury yourselves in scripture, service, and work, and you will bury this sin.

Finally, the prayer offered by Nephi at the passing of his father, Lehi, is more than just a moving scripture. It is the prayer that all of us should utter in our efforts to bury our sins, whatever they may be. "O Lord, wilt thou redeem my soul? Wilt thou deliver me out of the hands of mine enemies? Wilt thou make me that I may shake at the appearance of sin?" (2 Nephi 4:31). Here, Nephi prays not just for forgiveness but also for redemption, delivery, and a true change of heart, so that sin would no longer even be a temptation to him.

I truly believe this same blessing is available to us. If our hearts are in the right place, the Lord can give us not just the strength to overcome or resist but also the purity to make us shake at the appearance of this kind of sin. This means ultimately reaching the point where the temptation is no longer a temptation because the sin is so deeply buried.

You can do it. With your Guide, you can do it. I know. I have seen it.

DEBT

Prophets, seers, and revelators have spoken very plainly about the sad effects of debt in our lives and in our marriages. "Remember this: debt is a form of bondage. It is a financial termite. When we make purchases on credit, they give us only an illusion of prosperity. We think we own things, but the reality is, our things own us" (Joseph B. Wirthlin, "Earthly Debts, Heavenly Debts," *Ensign,* May 2005).

President N. Eldon Tanner taught, "I am convinced that it is not the amount of money an individual earns that brings peace of mind as much as it is having control of his money. Money can be an obedient servant but a harsh taskmaster. Those who structure their standard of living to allow a little surplus, control their circumstances. Those who spend a little more than they earn are controlled by their circumstances. They are in bondage" ("Constancy Amid Change," *Ensign,* November 1979).

And President Heber J. Grant taught directly, "If there is any one thing that will bring peace and contentment into the human heart, and into the family, it is to live within our means. And if there is any one thing that is grinding and discouraging and disheartening, it is to have debts and obligations that one cannot meet" ("Gospel Standards," *Improvement Era* [Salt Lake City: 1941], 111).

The Lord warns at least four times in the Doctrine and Covenants against debt. In fact, He commands against it and even calls it "bondage," a word we see in other prophetic teachings about debt (D&C 19:35; 64:27; 104:78; 115:13).

Debt intersects with gospel principles not just because it brings misery but also because it messes with our agency. For example, when we are indebted, our opportunities and agency are limited. My mission president years ago took the time to teach some of his missionaries about how debt can hurt. He told us about some great friends of his who would be wonderful assets to the Lord as mission presidents or General Authorities, but he said they were probably disqualified from service because of . . . debt. They were so steeped in debt that they would not be able to afford to leave their jobs and serve missions. I had never thought of it that way. But I'm grateful for the lesson. Debt disqualifies you from service opportunities.

Debt is the antithesis of self-reliance, a frequently taught gospel principle. "I am suggesting that the time has come to get our houses in order," President Gordon B. Hinckley urged Church members during the October 1998 general conference. "Self-reliance cannot obtain when there is serious debt hanging over a household. One has neither independence nor freedom from bondage when he is obligated to others" ("To the Boys and to the Men," *Ensign,* November 1998).

In marriages, debt hangs over the couple mercilessly. It leads to disagreements, disharmony, and a host of just plain stupid decisions. And, of course, bad decisions lead to debt. It's a vicious circle.

Debt can also drive people away from paying tithing. When faced with having a car repossessed or having utilities shut off, people often choose to let their tithing slide. We know how dangerous that is.

Threat Level: Ursula the Sea Witch

Debt also has a whole lot in common with Ursula the Sea Witch. She is a big, fat, mean octopus. She has a multitude of tentacles to grab you and hold on to you. She can give you something you want—a momentary pleasure or something big and shiny that you simply must have—but you will pay a huge price for it. That price gets more and more expensive each day. She will take much more than your voice.

Q: How can we avoid debt?

A: Don't buy things if you can't afford them.

I have noticed a few huge recurrences that lead to debt problems. First, I have seen never-ending mortgage problems in nearly every failed marriage. I think I have seen only a handful of divorcing couples who have *ever* paid off their mortgage. And that includes millionaires!

Of course, mortgages aren't inherently evil, but the way people use them can become painful. They refinance their homes regularly whenever their other debt rises too much. This is the epitome of being penny-wise and pound-foolish because they are essentially paying for their homes again and again. They already bought their homes once, but they keep paying for that home again and again when they refinance to take out whatever equity they can. This starts the meter running all over again, and keeps that debt alive and well for decades to come. Couples who keep doing this will never, ever pay off their mortgage.

There is one other way that recurring mortgages crush a family financially. Some people keep moving from house to house, every few years, simply because they are accustomed to moving. I am not talking about outgrowing a home when the family grows or moving because of job or family considerations; I am talking about always wanting a bigger or nicer home. I'm talking about keeping up with the Joneses. Even if people in this cycle reap a big profit selling their previous home, they still expand their debt. They still put off the glorious day of paying off their home by a few decades. Not to mention, they're paying seven percent or more of your equity to a realtor and title company every time they do this. And worse, when the economy inevitably hits a tough spot, far too many people end up losing their homes altogether. Many times, this could have been avoided by living within our means. Often, this means staying put and making do with what we already have.

There are definitely gospel principles at work when it comes to buying a home and minimizing debt. Make your home purchase a matter of sincere prayer and fasting. Go where the Lord wants you to go—where He will put your talents to the best use and where you will bless the ward.

Q: Are there any kinds of debt that are okay?

A: Yes. President Hinckley mentioned some kinds of approved debt.

Education and buying a home are approved debt according to President Hinckley. More precisely, he said "completing" an education, meaning we should pay as much as we can with cash. Here are his actual words. "I hasten to add that borrowing under some circumstances is necessary. Perhaps you need to borrow to complete your education. If you do, see that you pay it back. And do so promptly even at the sacrifice of some comforts that you might otherwise enjoy. You likely will have to borrow in securing a home. But be wise and do not go beyond your ability to pay" (*Teachings of Gordon B. Hinckley* [Salt Lake City: Bookcraft, 1997], 154).

These are the only types of approved debt President Hinckley mentioned. He spoke specifically and clearly against credit cards ("To the Boys and to the Men," *Ensign*, November 1988). Those are high standards for us to live up to, but they are the words of a prophet. And there is so much safety in the words of prophets.

Abuse and Adultery

I am relieved and grateful to report that physical abuse has been relatively rare in my practice. I will not pretend that it does not exist. The abuse cases I have had are tragic and disgusting. There is no excuse for it. Playing a 911 recording in court is an absolutely harrowing experience that I don't wish on anyone.

I am putting adultery in the same category because I believe these sins are on par with each other, or close to it, as the Lord sees it. I believe their impacts on a marriage are comparable as well.

> "*Men, take care not to make women weep, for God counts their tears.*"

—Thomas S. Monson
("That We May Touch Heaven," *Ensign*, November 1990)

Threat Level: Dragon

The fire-breathing dragon is the most ruthless and powerful threat on the journey to happily ever after. It can destroy entire villages and armies at a time.

Q: Are you talking about physical abuse? What about emotional or verbal abuse?

A: I'm talking about all kinds of abuse. Physical abuse is inexcusable but easier to define. Emotional and verbal abuse are more difficult to address, for a few different reasons. Hear me out.

Verbal abuse is covered in the discussion on unkind words. Make no mistake—this is often very real abuse. It requires immediate repentance. It causes tears, and God counts those tears.

Emotional abuse is actually very difficult to define. In clinical terms, at least under the law where I practice, emotional abuse means withholding necessities such as food, clothing, and shelter from children. I have seen cases where one parent's multiple false allegations of sexual abuse, including subjecting a child to invasive physical examinations, were found to be emotional abuse. Other than that, it's hard to get very definitive about emotional abuse. That means being a controlling, obnoxious, belittling, intolerable, wretched spouse would probably not rise to the level of what the law would consider abuse.

That's the law of man, though. The law of God would not tolerate anything of the sort. Any level of verbal or emotional mistreatment is a violation of covenants.

Because there are so many different levels of what might be considered emotional abuse, it's just too hard for me to comment on here. I would have to know the individual facts of the case to answer that question fully.

At the same time, I believe actual abuse is only slightly worse than false allegations of abuse. Check that—false allegations of abuse *are* abuse. In my practice, I have seen a great many more false allegations of child abuse than true allegations. These are the sickest divorces of all. The Savior has warned of terrible judgments for those who harm children (Matthew 18:6). I believe there will be similarly dreadful judgments for those who falsely allege such abuse. I am sure that God also counts the tears of the falsely accused.

That might be more than you wanted to hear, but I think it needed to be said. Bottom line: I can't split hairs about what does or does not rise to the level of emotional abuse. I believe the Lord would strongly admonish against "anything like unto" abuse. It does not have to be legally considered abuse to be sinful or to be a threat to happily ever after.

Q: You mention physical abuse out of other levels or types of abuse. What about unfaithfulness? It has different levels too.

A: Excellent point.

Adultery is the most severe level of unfaithfulness, but there are certainly other levels that are wrong and will lead to unhappiness. Pornography or any other lustful viewing or thought is clearly a level of unfaithfulness and is a violation of covenants. "Ye have heard that it was said by them of old time, Thou shalt not commit adultery: But I say unto you, That whosoever looketh on a woman to lust after her hath committed adultery with her already in his heart" (Matthew 5:28). D&C 42:23 and 63:16 teach the same lesson with a few more details about the consequences of lustful staring. This is definitely a level of infidelity that causes problems and cries out for repentance.

Flirting, inappropriate touching, inappropriate conversation, or just plain getting too close to a member of the opposite sex are all levels of the same greater sin.

Q: At what point is someone getting too close to a member of the opposite sex?

A: I have two answers to this question.

One, when your thoughts start to wander. Our thoughts go hand-in-hand with our words and our actions. Romantic or other thoughts that wander in the direction of another person who is not our spouse are wrong and harmful and have very real consequences. "For our words will condemn us, yea, all our works will condemn us; we shall not be found spotless; and our thoughts will also condemn us; and in this awful state we shall not dare to look up to our God; and we would fain be glad if we could command the rocks and the mountains to fall upon us to hide us from his presence" (Alma 12:14). Stop the pattern at or before your thoughts, and you'll never have to worry about any condemnation beyond that.

In a sad reminder of the consequences of where unclean thoughts lead, President Gordon B. Hinckley taught, "I remember going to President McKay years ago to plead the cause of a missionary who had become involved in serious sin. I said to President McKay, 'He did it on an impulse.' The President said to me: 'His mind was dwelling on these things before he transgressed. The thought was father to the deed. There would not have been that impulse if he had previously controlled his thoughts'" ("Be Ye Clean," *Ensign,* May 1996).

The second answer about when you're getting too friendly with a member of the opposite sex is simple: If your spouse is uncomfortable with your level of friendship with a member of the opposite sex, then you should be uncomfortable with it too. Time to stop.

Final Thoughts on Abuse and Adultery

Earlier, we talked about the dangers of covenant drift and ending up in the adversary's power. Abuse and adultery represent a nearly complete delivery into the adversary's hands. This level of sin doesn't happen on a whim. I view these problems as products— as symptoms—more than causes. They build up from unkind words, a sense of self-righteousness, and so many other problems we've discussed in this book. These are the culmination of so many of those problems. These are the worst that can happen when other problems are allowed to fester.

When I stated that these problems are (thankfully) relatively rare in my experience, that may well be because one spouse taps out of the marriage before these problems reach this level. That doesn't make abuse and adultery any less of a sin or a tragedy; it emphasizes the importance of capping the other problems before they reach this level. You can do it. I have seen the power of the Guide to help you do it.

Untreated
Mental Illness

Let me say this as clearly as I know how to say it: There is no shame in having a mental illness. The shame is in not treating it. That is when it becomes truly debilitating.

Mental illness, for the most part, is very survivable in a marriage, as long as it is treated. In my experience, spouses of mentally ill people dearly love their spouses and would do anything to help them. It is when the person refuses help or refuses to acknowledge the illness that things go south.

It can also become a problem when a spouse tries to use it as a free-pass excuse for life. This is wrong. You were not placed on earth to fail. You can still live a good life and bless many people in spite of your illness. In fact, you'd be amazed how many people in your same boat you can bless *because* of your illness. You can still have a wonderful marriage in spite of your illness if you will treat it.

In a very real way, the problem feeds itself. People are so concerned with the stigma of having a mental illness that they deny they have it. Then they quit treating, and they spiral downward.

Maybe if we could remove some of the stigma that surrounds mental illness, we could solve this problem.

This much I can tell you: Whenever someone says he or she can handle it without anybody's help, that someone will fail. It's the same with addiction. The surest way to fail with a problem of this nature is to deny having it or to think that you have it under control all on your own. In either case, you're wrong. The problem will not take care of itself. You have to admit it and tackle it head on, or it will tackle you. I have argued this many times to judges in custody disputes, and my experience is that judges agree.

"You don't have to prove nothin' to nobody. Just take good care of yourself."

—Don Henley

Now, this works both ways. If the spouse suffering the illness can't live in denial of it, then neither can the other spouse. It is an illness. It is real. It is not something that can be prayed away. It is not something that some degree of optimism or faith can magically make disappear.

I came to learn more than I ever wanted to learn about this subject when I was put on cancer medication and the side effects flattened me, physically and mentally. These drugs were literally designed to remix my body's chemistry to fight the cancer. And they do exactly that. In remixing the chemistry, they did a lot more than fight cancer. They gave me severe depression. If I had ever been a naysayer or a minimizer on the subject of mental illness before, I apologize.

On behalf of many, many people who have suffered and have been told that it's all in their head or that they just need to exercise some faith, please indulge this rant. Can I just say how demoralizing it is to hear someone suggest that more prayer or scripture reading will solve the problem? Can I just say how much it *doesn't* help to have someone suggest that it's all in your head and just a little bit of willpower can overcome it?

Please, don't ever tell anyone that prayer or fasting will solve their depression. Of course you mean well, but those comments just make it worse. They need love and support, not advice from someone who doesn't even speak the same language.

Bottom line: No spouse and no family member can afford to live in denial of mental illness. If it is treated with medicine, compassion, and charity, it is survivable in your marriage. If it is not, then you can't expect the marriage to thrive.

Threat Level:
Broken vessel

Elder Jeffrey R. Holland's landmark conference address on mental illness is so appropriately named "Like a Broken Vessel" (*Ensign*, November 2013). When this vessel (think: the car you are driving or the horse you are riding) breaks down in the middle of the journey and in the middle of nowhere, you feel stranded. You're miles from anywhere and certainly miles from safety. You feel like easy prey for all the dangerous wild animals around you, not to mention the suddenly scorching sun. Every little sound you hear makes you flinch. You're convinced it's a lion ready to pounce on you, even if it's just a grasshopper. All you want is someone to come and rescue you. You don't care about taking in any more sights on this journey. You're not enjoying it at all. You just want some relief.

Q: What kind of treatment is needed?

A: My own experience tells me . . .

Physical activity is the only relief from depression that I've found. The problem is, it is really, really hard to get up and go running or do anything when you feel like a melted candle.

Please understand, this is only *my* experience, and it is only with one form of mental illness, namely depression. I won't try to diagnose any other forms or recommend any treatment for them because I just don't know.

When in doubt, seek professional attention.

WHAT ABOUT ADDICTION?

Q: Wait, you didn't mention addiction in your most common pitfalls. Doesn't alcohol destroy more marriages than anything else?

A: Yes, addiction destroys countless marriages.

But this problem is 100% avoidable thanks to the Word of Wisdom. The Lord knew exactly what He was doing in giving that commandment. Simple as that.

And If We Don't Survive the Journey to Happily Ever After?

I f you end up in the heartbreaking position of going through a divorce, please let me offer a few words based on my experience to help you. (You might want to skip this chapter unless it applies to you. Or maybe, just maybe, if you read this section, it might help you rework some things and save the marriage.)

Q: How do I know when it's time to call it quits?

A: Nobody can answer that question for you.

It is your agency, and it's your marriage.

I know that's not what you want to hear, so let me share with you a few more specific thoughts. I learned early on being a lawyer that there was only one way to live with myself in this profession. I hate losing, but, as my favorite law professor taught, any lawyer who hasn't lost a lot of cases hasn't had a lot of cases. Family lawyers don't work with just contracts, boring documents, or other stuff; they work with families.

So, how did I learn to live with that kind of pressure when I knew I wasn't going to win them all? The only way to do it was to know that I had truly given it my best effort.

The same thing goes for marriage. The only way to live with yourself if you are going to get divorced is to know that you truly gave it your best effort to save the marriage. It is nothing to be taken lightly or to be decided quickly. Most of your thought process on the subject will consist of reviewing everything you've done and questioning if you have truly given it your best effort.

> *"To give anything less than your best is to sacrifice the gift."*
>
> —Steve Prefontaine

Remember the question repeated time and again throughout this book—"Lord, is it I?" Nowhere is that question more important than with this subject. Your sacrifice must be truly acceptable to the Lord before going to this point.

Q: What about abuse and adultery? Aren't they enough to call it quits unquestionably?

A: No, not always.

In years past, when I knew a lot less but thought I knew a lot more than I do now, I would have answered this question "absolutely." But since then, I've seen marriages heal, even from these terrible things. I will not counsel anyone to stay in a truly abusive marriage, but I've seen very good people—people I genuinely love—climb out of the deepest of these pitfalls. You can never bank on this, but I will say that I have seen it happen.

Remember the Atonement. It is the only cure for the attack of this dragon.

Maybe you have noticed something—throughout all the pitfalls and their threat levels, the Guide never leaves. He never quits. You might have separated yourself from Him, but He never gives up on you.

Q: What if I want to reconcile, but he (or she) doesn't?

A: The only way to repair a broken relationship is to soften the heart.

A broken relationship does not heal without a complete and mutual surrender. Both hearts must be softened. If you are looking for a specific prayer to offer, it would be that the Lord would soften somebody's heart. This requires divine intervention to cut through someone's pain, and that is not easy. Hardened hearts do not want to change. That may be because of pride, but it also may be a survival instinct. The heart has been broken, and it doesn't want to open itself up to breaking again. Only the Living Savior, who has carried all our sorrows and griefs, can heal and soften a heart.

When the heart has simply been broken, trust has to be rebuilt. That requires an all-out effort.

When the heart is clamped shut because of pride, that requires the mutual surrender mentioned above. It requires both parties to completely drop their positions about who was right and who was wrong. Remember, "Pride does not look up to God and care about what is right. It looks sideways to man and argues who is right" (Ezra Taft Benson, "Cleansing the Inner Vessel," *Ensign*, May 1989). At this stage, neither party can dig in and place any blame on the other. The only desire either can have is to reconcile, to bury any ill feelings, and to never speak of them again. The ego has to be set aside completely. Mercy has to flourish in both spouses. That is a huge part of what it means to soften a heart.

> *"Why don't we both surrender before we both get burned?"*
>
> —Bourgeois Tagg

Can this really happen? Yes. And it is a beautiful thing. The switch can be flipped. Enemies can become the best of friends in an instant. I have seen it. I have lived it, just not in the context of a marriage. But it only happens though mighty prayer, a mutual surrender, and two softened hearts. It is the exception, not the rule.

Q: And if we do end up in a divorce, what advice can you give?

A: My motto is that pain is inevitable but misery is optional. Here's my list of things to minimize pain and hopefully avoid misery.

1. **Understand that most divorces really, truly should settle without going to trial.**

   I would say 90 to 95% of family law cases really should settle (even though they don't). You will almost always be happier in the long run if you settle. The time, money, and heartache you will save by settling your case is incalculable.

2. **Your case can only settle if you're both reasonable and willing to compromise.**

You never get everything you're looking for by going to court. It just doesn't happen. You have to prioritize what means the most to you and pick your battles based on your priorities. You will have to be reasonable. And maybe, if you are good at making compromises, you could call off the divorce altogether and save your marriage.

3. **You can't afford to have a sense of entitlement.**

You may feel like he or she just plain "owes" you. You may be very well justified in feeling this way, but it won't help you get through the divorce, and it sure won't help you heal afterward. Instead, it will keep you miserable for a very long time because you will likely never feel that you have gotten all that you truly deserve. A sense of entitlement is a surefire recipe for misery, both in marriage and in divorce.

4. **Do not try to make it a holy war.**

Wars fought "in the name of God" have claimed millions of lives throughout history. You cannot think of your divorce as a holy war.

The court system is a system of man, not of God. Your judge is a very imperfect person who makes mistakes. Your ultimate Judge is perfect and very different. That is the only judgment where you can count on perfect justice and true mercy.

5. **Do not turn children into property.**

The most surefire way I know of to be miserable in a family court action—for you, your spouse, and your children—is to turn your children into pawns. Your spouse does not have to earn the right to parent from you. Your children are people, and people are not property. One of my favorite professors at BYU referred to the phenomenon of turning people into property as "the Mahanic principle," after Cain's self-given title.

Cain sought to turn his brother Abel's life into his own worldly gain. He went as far as to kill his brother to carry out this plan. When people in court try to turn human beings—their own children, no less—into property, they are committing a grievous sin. Your children are not a means to an end. They are not property to be turned against either of their parents. They are children. Your duty is to care for them, not to use them against their father or mother. It is difficult enough to raise children with two parents. Why would you want to push one of the parents out of the picture and try to do it solo if you can possibly avoid it?

6. **Work with an eye toward healing.**

You have to heal. That takes time. It takes forgiveness. It takes a softened heart. It takes letting go and forgetting about who is right. It takes a genuine desire to heal. And it takes time. The good news is that, unlike a courtroom scenario, there is all sorts of divine intervention available when your goal is truly to heal.

What Can We Teach Our Children to Help Them Have a Happy Marriage?

Q: Let's start with the biggie. What is the most important thing to teach children to help them become good spouses?

A: Teach them the plan of salvation. Start by teaching them the reality of the Atonement of Jesus Christ.

Good parents take advantage of every opportunity to teach the plan of salvation to their children. They hold family home evening each week. They read scriptures and pray as a family every day. They take advantage of the countless teaching moments that come in everyday life. They teach by precept— meaning actual face-to-face teaching like the examples just mentioned—and by example. They live the gospel themselves, and their children learn endlessly from their example.

In particular, good parents teach the reality of the Savior's Atonement. I have had lots of clients divorce bad spouses. What I mean is, many times these bad spouses were bad from the beginning, so bad that the client had to know heading into the marriage that this was not going to be a good spouse. More than once, I have asked the question, "Why did you marry him (or her) in the first place?" The answer surprised me. I expected to hear, "I thought I could change him (or her)." In second place, I expected to hear, "I was young and immature." Somewhere in there, I thought for sure I would at least hear, "I don't know." I don't think I've heard one of those answers yet.

The answer I get has been, "I didn't think I could do any better." Usually, the complete answer is something along the lines of, "I messed up, so I didn't think I could do any better."

This is tragic. It does not have to be that way. This mindset is nothing more than a misunderstanding of our divine nature and of the Atonement of Jesus Christ.

Our children are not just our children, they are God's children, and the worth of a child of God is infinite. That infinite worth is attained through the Atonement of Jesus Christ. With remarkably few exceptions, any sin can be fully, completely, and thoroughly cleansed. No sin is beyond the Savior's reach to take away.

One of my favorite lessons on the Atonement comes from its Hebrew meaning. The word *kaphar* (you might recognize it in another form as *kippur*, as in Yom Kippur, the Day of Atonement) is remarkable and sweeping in its meanings and applications. It means to appease, to cover, to cleanse, to pardon, to pacify, to purge, to put off, to reconcile, to be merciful toward, to forgive, and to disannul. Is there any comfort or any blessing missing in that definition? It's beautiful. It's real. That's the Atonement.

That last definition—to disannul—is especially intriguing. *Webster's* defines it as a complete or utter annulment. There are no remnants or traces left. It's gone completely. The strict etymology of the word suggests something even more interesting. The Latin prefix "dis" indicates a negative or reversing force. In this sense, a "disannulment" would be a double negative, a reversal of a reversal. Applied to the Atonement, this may be the most beautiful double negative you will ever find. By this strict etymology definition, the Atonement exists to undo our undoing. When we feel or believe we are undone, the Atonement undoes the undoing we feel. Our children cannot afford to grow up believing that any sin is beyond the reach of the Savior to undo. By either definition of "disannul," it is possible to remove not just the sin, but any trace of it.

The sin may require the help of a bishop who holds the keys of gospel of repentance in your ward. And what a beautiful blessing those keys are. Welcome those keys and pay the price. It is not just the Atonement available to us; it is the power of the Living Christ. He is mighty to save, and He wants nothing more than to save. We can rest assured that Heavenly Father will apply the greatest mercy possible under all the circumstances. That mercy comes through the Living Savior and His Atonement. You don't need to "settle" because of your sins if those sins are truly behind you. And they can indeed be put behind you once and for all.

Q: What else do we need to teach our children to help them prepare for a happy marriage?

A: Teach them how to pray and how to recognize answers from the Lord.

Choosing a spouse is the biggest choice you will make in mortality. You don't make a choice like that without asking the Lord for guidance. We ask for advice from a trusted person about where to go to school, what job to take, and countless other questions. Those questions are important and even huge, but they are not nearly as important or as huge as the choice of a spouse. Just as we would ask advice of a trusted friend, a teacher, or a parent, we have a perfect and all-knowing Heavenly Father we should ask about this most important choice. We do that through prayer.

The catch is, we have to know how the Lord speaks to us in order to receive that advice. We have to recognize the voice and promptings of the Holy Ghost, as He is the Lord's voice to us. This becomes even more difficult because the feelings of the Spirit tend to feel a lot like the feeling of being in love. We have to be able to tell the difference between our own emotions and twitterpation and the voice of the Lord.

President Kimball taught, "In selecting a companion for life and for eternity, certainly the most careful planning and thinking and praying and fasting should be done to be sure that, of all the decisions, this one must not be wrong. In true marriage there must be a union of minds as well as of hearts. Emotions must not wholly determine decisions, but the mind and the heart, strengthened by fasting and prayer and serious consideration, will give one a maximum chance of marital happiness" ("Marriage and Divorce," [Brigham Young University devotional, Sept. 7, 1976]).

To make things more difficult, many of our children—too many of our children—don't truly and earnestly seek answers to prayers until they look for the Lord's guidance on this most important question. This is like picking up a football for the first time when you're playing quarterback in the Super Bowl. Our children might dream of playing in the Super Bowl, but even when they're dreaming, they know that they have to put in years and years of practice and hone their skills to their absolute peak if they're actually going to do it.

So how do we give them years and years of practice in recognizing the voice of the Lord before this Super Bowl of life called marriage? Teach them by precept and example. Precept means you teach them face to face, as you would in family home evenings, in daily scripture study (yes, in addition to the study with your spouse, mentioned previously), and in countless other teaching moments that arise. Teach them the fruits of the Spirit and remind them that those fruits can be mistaken for our own emotions without a lot of experience. Bear testimony to them of gospel truths and point out the presence of the Spirit, because if you feel that presence, they most likely feel it too. Share personal experiences of how the Lord answered your prayers of direction. Share stories in the scriptures and in the lives of faithful saints who have acted on promptings. There will always be at least one talk at every general conference that offers insights on hearing the Lord's voice. Make those talks a huge priority as you review conference talks, especially as your children reach their teens and late teens. President Dallin H. Oaks in particular has spoken on the subject many times. His talks and articles are a great resource on the subject.

Missionary service also provides many priceless opportunities to learn to recognize answers to prayers. This should not be the main reason anyone serves a mission, but serving a mission is certainly a prime opportunity to learn to recognize the voice of Lord on a regular basis. Countless blessings come from consecrating eighteen months or two years to the Lord by serving a mission, but the blessing of hearing and following the promptings of the Holy Ghost would make the whole mission worth every minute of work and sacrifice.

Teach them that inspiration comes in different ways. My mission president taught this lesson by sharing his experience as an assistant to two different presidents. His first mission president began the process by kneeling down in prayer and asking for the Lord's guidance as he moved missionaries around the board to the right area. In contrast, his second mission president began the process by going right to the board and moving around the missionaries. This caught him off guard, and he wondered why the process didn't start with a prayer. No worries. After he had a tentative plan for each of his missionaries, this mission president reverently dropped to his knees, pleaded for the Lord to confirm that the right choices had been made and that any corrections needed would be inspired. Both approaches sought the Lord's voice, and both worked.

I don't mind sharing my own experience with this Super Bowl of all questions. After spending lots of time with her and her family, and having her meet my family, I felt great about marrying Cami. I had fought it for a while, but it was clear she was determined to follow the Lord, that she came from a great family, and that we were just plain happy together. I had a pretty strong feeling that I would be a fool to let her get away. This was my way of arranging the board beforehand, much like the mission president in the example above. It was my way of "study[ing] it out" in my mind before asking the Lord (D&C 9:8).

With that in mind, I took the question to the Lord about whether I should ask her to marry me. As I stayed on my knees and listened and watched for impressions to come to me, my mind was filled with visions of Cami as a very old lady. She was recognizable, but she was very wrinkled, very gray, old, and still very, very beautiful to me. I found myself smiling as these visions came to me. I asked myself, "Do I still love this ninety-year-old Cami?" Absolutely I did. That was my answer. It was not at all what I expected, but it was my answer. I knew the Lord had spoken to me. And boy am I glad I acted on it.

But I didn't stop asking because, remember, the Lord teaches us line upon line. Some time later, Cami flew out to join my family on a vacation in Del Mar, California. On the beach at what was supposed to be sunset, we went for a walk. "Will you do me a favor?" I asked her. "Sure." "Try this on and tell me if you'll marry me," I said, as I pulled the diamond ring out of my pocket. She said yes, even if it took a few seconds that seemed like forever. I'm smiling just thinking about it.

When she had to fly back to Utah, and we had said goodbye, I knelt down again and asked the Lord to confirm the decision I'd made—if I should stay this course, like the mission president who had arranged the board and asked for a confirmation afterward. The answer to this latest prayer was more like what I had expected before. The Spirit came over me so strongly that I bawled. Through my sobs, I found myself saying out loud, "I could not have asked for anything more."

I look back on both of those prayer answers regularly. They're treasures to me. They are anchors whenever a storm hits, because life throws all sorts of storms at any marriage. The Lord spoke to me in two very different and distinct ways. I had to be familiar with His voice in order to recognize those answers.

The Lord speaks in different ways to different people. We have to be able to hear and understand those promptings, and we have to teach our children to do the same. My friends, this is not optional. Our children absolutely must have experiences in recognizing the Lord's voice to them before they come to Him with the most important question of all.

Q: What else do we need to teach children on this subject?

A: Teach them to start early on to have and keep the Holy Ghost as their constant companion throughout their relationship.

Earlier I stressed the importance of starting off a marriage—starting off an engagement, actually—by reading scriptures and praying together daily. I called it the single best piece of marriage advice I'd ever received. What makes it so great? It invites the Holy Ghost into the relationship every single day. You can't go through marriage without this representative of the Godhead.

One of the saddest and most difficult problems to overcome in a marriage is when a couple is married in the temple without being properly prepared. And by "prepared," I mean, among other things, worthy. I remember well the words of a religion professor I had at BYU, who talked about his engagement with his wife. Richard Draper told us with a gleam in his eye about how much he loved his wife, and how that gleam found a permanent home when they were first engaged. They were affectionate, but they knew where to draw the line. Because of that, the Spirit was always part of their relationship. When people start off on the wrong foot by hurrying to the temple when they're not ready, they never give the Holy Ghost that same chance that Brother Draper and his wife had to be their constant companion in their marriage.

Some couples feel social pressure, first to be married in the temple and then to keep a scheduled date if something bad happens or if they're otherwise unprepared for the ordinances of the temple. If announcements have been made or mailed, the thought or embarrassment of not following through can be

WHAT CAN WE TEACH OUR CHILDREN?

overwhelming. But the consequences of entering the temple unworthily are much more painful, even though they aren't publicized. Starting off marriage on this wrong note is something that many couples never recover from. Please, please trust me on this. It is far better to call off a wedding, postpone a wedding, or perform the wedding outside of the temple than it is to enter the temple unworthily. We all know that two wrongs don't make a right, and this is a whole different level of wrongs here. Just like the ability to recognize answers to your prayers, the presence of the Holy Ghost in your marriage is not optional. You do not want to live without this blessing.

Q: Is there anything else we should teach our children about marriage?

A: Teach them by example.

You are teaching your children every day of your marriage, whether you realize it or not. You are teaching them by example in everything you do. Please, make sure that example you are setting is a good one. (A sincere and eternal thank you to my own parents, especially my father, who gave me a daily example of a righteous husband and father. You did marvelously well.)

Q: What are the warning signs of a bad future spouse?

A: They are the problems that are not likely to change during the marriage.

You've probably heard that a girl should look for a guy who treats his mother well. That is a wonderful starting point. It really is great advice on what to look for. It's just not enough.

Girls, you've probably heard that you want to look for a guy who is good with children. That's also great advice. And also not nearly enough.

It's always good to be an optimist, but in this business of marriage and eternity, you need to keep your eyes and your heart open to the negative. You have to look for things to avoid.

The best way to answer this question about warning signs might be to point out ways in which someone is unlikely to change. No doubt, we can and should hope to grow and improve throughout our years on earth. That's what mortality is for, after all. Still, you can never plan on changing someone during marriage, and some characteristics are especially unlikely to change. In fact, these major warning signs are problems that are more likely to get worse during marriage, not better. During marriage, both good and bad traits tend to be amplified.

In my experience and study, here are some of the bad things that are unlikely to improve.

1. Not joining the Church

Statistically speaking, non-members are very unlikely to join the Church in marriage. The best lesson on this subject I know of comes from a book called *Teens, Temple Marriage, and Eternity* by Allan K. Burgess. He compares the likelihood of a non-member joining the Church after marriage to the odds of surviving a game of Russian roulette.

Many members of the Church play a variation of Russian roulette called "he (or she) isn't a member of the Church yet, but I know that he (or she) will join after we get married." This game has odds that are even less appealing than Russian roulette, and most people don't like the way it ends, either. President Spencer W. Kimball gave the odds for this very dangerous game:

Surveys have indicated that only one of seven finally joins the Church—the odds are against the others. And nearly half of those who marry out of the Church become inactive. As parents give up their religion, an increasing number of their children are brought up without any religion.

So you are taking a desperate chance if you say, "Well, maybe he will join after we are married. We will go ahead and try it and see." It is a pretty serious thing to take a chance on. ("The Importance of Celestial Marriage," *Ensign*, October 1979)

If we marry out of the Church, we have only about a 14 percent chance of ending up with an eternal marriage. When we make this decision, in all reality, we are playing Russian roulette with our exaltation.

President Kimball also spoke of two other side effects of marrying out of the Church: half of those who are active slip into inactivity, and numerous children are brought up without the gospel. In effect, we play Russian roulette with our children's lives as well. The attitude of "We will be able to go to the temple someday" leads to much heartbreak and sorrow. It is nothing more than rationalization and procrastination.

Q: How do you avoid this?

A: Don't seriously date someone who isn't within close reach of temple worthiness.

Just don't go there. This is why *For the Strength of Youth* speaks so clearly on the subject. "As you enter your adult years, make dating and marriage a high priority. Seek a companion who is worthy to go to the temple to be sealed to you for time and all eternity. Marrying in the temple and creating an eternal family are essential in God's plan of happiness." (*For the Strength of*

Youth, Dating section) Of course, people who are not members of the Church can't hold a temple recommend. The eternal blessings of the temple are not available to them or to the family as a whole.

You can never plan on changing someone through marriage. The odds of being able to change someone in this department are too grim to play with. I know plenty of very, very good people who have married outside of the Church. They have given it a valiant effort, to be sure. But sadly, most of them fall right in line with this statistic. It's hard enough raising children in today's world, and these good, good people face extra challenges in raising their children in the gospel without the help of the other parent. You just can't plan on changing someone to be baptized and to embrace the blessings of the Restoration and the temple. Teach your children not to head down this path, because the odds are overwhelming that it will not take them to an eternal marriage.

2. Lacking commitment to the gospel

I don't have statistics to apply to this one, but it is similarly real. So many failed marriages never truly get off on the right foot because the spouses have very different levels of commitment to the gospel. Again, we all hope to improve our commitment and worthiness, but many differences in potential spouses' commitment levels are obvious from the beginning. This difference grows wider and wider like a wedge throughout a marriage. It gets even more divisive when children are in the home. Disputes come up about raising these children in a gospel-centered home. Those disputes all too easily and frequently drive couples to the marriage mortician. You can't plan on changing this commitment level.

Q: So, how do we spot this lack of commitment problem early on?

A: Suggestion number one: Sister missionaries tend to be especially strong.

Please understand that these are observations and suggestions based on my experience. They are not hard and fast "rules," and they certainly can't be taken as guarantees. Having said that, let me start by saying that, in my experience, sister missionaries have a stronger tendency to remain strong in the Church than do men.

Years ago, a good friend of mine told me, "I'm tired of telling girls to look for a returned missionary to marry. I've seen too many returned missionaries go bad." Unfortunately, he's right. I can't endorse the status of a returned missionary as a litmus test for a good husband who will remain fully committed to the gospel. It is helpful, but it does not necessarily mean that the man is firmly on the strait and narrow.

However, I will say that I have seen very few returned sister missionaries go less active. So while I can't endorse the returned missionary litmus test for elders, I can endorse it for returned missionary sisters. Obviously, no measure is perfect because everyone has agency, and that is the great wild card in the plan of salvation. Still, guys, if you find a returned sister missionary who served honorably, the odds are very strong that you indeed have a keeper. This doesn't mean that you should dump a girl if she's not a returned missionary, by any means; it just means that sister missionaries are awesome, and they tend to stay awesome.

Q: What else is a good predictor
of staying strong?

A: Suggestion number two: Don't underestimate
the value of seminary in someone's youth.

For other predictors of who will stay strong, I have some limited
experience that might be helpful. It comes from the ward I grew
up in. It was a fantastic ward, one of the greatest in the whole
Church, I believe. We had thirteen active deacons at one point—
so many that we couldn't all pass the sacrament. As our group got
older and became teachers and then priests, though, only five of
us ended up serving a mission. Those are the same five who are
still active today.

Thinking about this, the sociology major in me took over,
and I began to analyze my old friends' circumstances to see what
I could learn. I broke down all the common factors to see what
it was that made the difference in our group of five. I analyzed
who had active parents, who came from part-member families,
who were Eagle Scouts, and every other category I could think
of and knew about. (Disclaimer: I don't know whose parents had
daily scripture study and prayer in their families and held family
home evening each week. That would have been extremely helpful to know, but we will just have to leave that factor out of the
equation.) There was one common factor that all five shared: We
all graduated from seminary. When I shared this experience with
a ward council, some other members of the ward council ran the
same informal analysis and found the same conclusion. Seminary
graduation was the one common theme that set everyone on the
path from which they did not stray.

Now, I haven't interviewed divorce clients about who graduated from seminary and who didn't, but my experience is strong

enough to convince me of the importance of seminary. There is something about the daily sacrifice of getting up at 5 a.m. or so to attend seminary or fit in another class during the school year or during the summer that molds someone for better things. I can't recommend seminary strongly enough. I plead with you to make seminary a priority for your children. It will do wonders to keep them strong their whole lives and to be righteous and good parents and spouses.

Q: What other indicators are there?

A: Suggestion number three: Find a good woman and marry her daughter.

This is one of the greatest pieces of advice you'll find. It came to me via my dear friend David Linford, whose father, Ray, taught it to him. Find a good woman and marry her daughter. Daughters tend to be a lot like their mothers. Of course, you will need to spend some time around your potential spouse and his or her parents to gauge if the apple has fallen far from the tree (and sometimes it's a good thing for apples to fall far from the tree). But this one worked for me. My mother-in-law is one of the most Christlike people I've ever known, and one of the things that first attracted me to Cami was her wonderful family. This is a solid piece of advice here, friends.

Yes, sons tend to be a lot like their fathers, but probably not as much as daughters tend to be like their mothers.

Q: Any other clues on what to look for?

A: Suggestion number four: There is no substitute for experience, no counterfeit for prayer, and no gift quite like the gift of discernment.

In gauging someone's level of future commitment to living the Gospel, there is no substitute for time and experience. You have to spend time together in lots of different circumstances. This is a huge reason why you can't rush into commitment. I'm sure it's a big part of why short courtships tend to end in divorces. And, of course, LDS courtships tend to be shorter than average. The Lord expects you to study things out in your own mind before coming to Him in prayer (D&C 9:7–9). Spending significant time with someone is a crucial part of the process of studying it out in your mind first.

Finally, couples have to communicate openly on this subject. I think any potential spouse has to ask openly and without hesitation about the other potential spouse's level of commitment. Actual questions on this subject are extremely helpful. Any list of questions that couples should ask each other before marriage should definitely emphasize this subject if they want to have a strong marriage.

Several pages back, I talked about reading and praying together as a couple during marriage. Try bringing up that suggestion before marriage and see how they respond. You can tell a whole lot about someone's spiritual depth by how he or she prays. You can get a similar picture by discussing gospel and scripture study topics beforehand.

Talk openly about spiritual goals you have, such as defining what regular temple attendance means to each of you.

You can also tell a whole lot about someone's spiritual depth by how he or she treats sacred things. The temple garment and the Sabbath come to mind. The temple garment is obviously a sacred thing, a reminder of our temple covenants. We have talked about how wearing or not wearing the garment properly is a barometer of your spiritual health. Likewise, the Sabbath is a sacred time. Those who treat it sacredly are more likely to maintain their spiritual commitment and build on it in the future.

And finally, this subject comes back to the issue of prayer, specifically your own prayer. Ask Heavenly Father for help seeing into your loved one's soul. Ask to see and recognize clues on this of all subjects. This is a gift of the Spirit that the Lord wants to give you. (See D&C 46, 1 Corinthians 15, and Moroni 10, as well as the importance of recognizing answers to prayer discussed previously.)

3. Controlling behavior

Someone who enters a relationship exhibiting controlling behavior is extremely unlikely to change. In fact, this behavior is only likely to get worse during a marriage. At least every week, clients tell me that their ex or soon-to-be ex is a master manipulator. He or she can be a real charmer but is actually a very different person underneath. We have probably all known someone like this. Many times, this mirage persona is a control freak. That obsession for control spirals out of control during the marriage, and the marriage can't survive. (See sections on self-righteousness and selfishness.)

Q: How do you spot controlling behavior ahead of time and avoid the misery that comes with it?

A: Here are some great questions to ask yourself:

+ Do they require you to account for where you are constantly?
+ Do they control or regularly ask how you spend your money?
+ Do they act as if you're accountable to them for your time, etc.?
+ Do they always have to be right?
+ Do they have a vocal opinion on just about everything, even trivial things?
+ Do they insist on doing things their way, even with simple things like which route to drive to get somewhere?
+ Do they always or almost always dictate your date activities without your input?
+ Do they pay attention when you speak your mind on something? Do they dismiss or laugh off your opinion when you do speak your mind? Do they make you feel like your opinion or your experience matters?
+ Do they use lines like "Aren't you glad you did it my way?" or "I told you . . ."?
+ Do they get jealous when you spend time with your friends?
+ Do they insult you?

You get the picture. These are big warning signs, especially when it comes to your friends or your money. Yes, you need to be realistic about finances together, but financial control will only grow thicker during the marriage. If you truly make financial decisions together, then you're okay. If one person is dictating the terms unilaterally, don't expect it to change. Expect it to be a serious problem.

If they are jealous of your time with your friends, that jealousy will expand to include your family. That will drive a wedge in the marriage, no doubt, and it will involve your whole family in the dispute. Marriages can then end up like family feuds.

But before you pull the plug, talk openly and politely about this. Don't accuse; just say, "Hey, I feel like you're asking too much about . . ." or "It feels condescending when you . . ." People can't be offended if you phrase your concern in terms of how you feel. It diffuses problems. It may be that someone is just following somebody else's example and doesn't even recognize what he or she is doing. If that person apologizes, takes constructive advice, and commits to change, then it's worth giving a chance. If the person gets defiant or worse, then you probably have an even stronger indicator that the person will not change.

This is extremely serious stuff here. Control too often becomes abuse within marriage. A temper too often becomes . . . well, worse. This is a huge warning sign.

People who are controlling can change, but they need to do it on their own time, not on your time during marriage. My advice is to run from anyone exhibiting controlling behavior if they don't change immediately. They can change, but they are very unlikely to change during marriage.

Now, if you find yourself answering any of those questions in the affirmative about yourself, then *you* need to change. If you are already married, then you need to change immediately. Recognizing the problem is always the first step to fixing it, so I take my hat off to you if you see and admit the problem in yourself.

4. Untreated mental illness

I want to be as clear as I possibly can be on this: There is no shame in mental illness. Not one ounce. The mind is susceptible to problems like any other organ in the body. The shame about mental illness lies in failing to acknowledge or treat the problems.

Untreated mental illness gets its own chapter in this book, where I talk about the most common pitfalls that doom marriages. The subject comes up here because mental illness is often, but certainly not always, known before the marriage. You do not and should not run from most mental illnesses before marriage if they are recognized and treated. Because the mind is by far the most complicated organ in the body, you wouldn't want to ignore its health any more than you would want to ignore the signs of a heart attack. You act to address the problem.

I repeat: Mental illness is no more shameful than a bad heart or a broken arm. If it is dealt with openly and treated earnestly, it should not be a marriage breaker. If it is not dealt with, it is often fatal to a marriage. Be as open about your mental health heading into marriage as you would be a bad heart or a broken arm. Do not put off or minimize treatment. Please.

5. Drama overload

The clinical term for this is a histrionic personality. In more familiar terms, it's a drama queen, except that guys can be this way too. Histrionic people thrive on conflict. They overreact, as if every sentence has to end in an exclamation point and every text or email should be in all caps. These people tend to be easily offended, and that does not work out well in marriage, where there are all sorts of opportunities to be offended, living every day with imperfect people. These people tend to love gossip. Perhaps the most difficult personality trait is that they embrace a victim mentality. In my experience, it is impossible to please

WHAT CAN WE TEACH OUR CHILDREN?

people who love to play the victim. They will always find something to be offended about. These people can mellow over time, but they usually have to get tired of being offended first. That's a level of self-awakening that you can only count on in yourself, not somebody else.

Q: What questions should you ask yourself when looking for a future spouse?

A: Besides keeping an eye out for the things that are unlikely to change, here are a few suggestions:

1. How does he or she treat you?

This is the simplest analysis of all. How does your possible future partner treat you? It seems obvious, so obvious that it gets overlooked sometimes. This characteristic is not likely to change dramatically. Again, rough edges can be smoothed off, but you can't expect a dramatic change.

"Be excellent to each other."

—Bill S. Preston, Esquire,
and Ted "Theodore" Logan

And let me be very clear about this: You can't get an accurate reading on this subject in any kind of short span. False charm can stick around a long time. You have to be in enough experiences and spend enough time with each other before getting married to see through any potential façade.

2. Does he or she make you want to be a better person?

There is a movie line I just love. The character is a self-centered, obsessive-compulsive wreck. But toward the end of the movie, he unleashes what I consider to be one of the sweetest compliments a guy can give. "You make me want to be a better man."

I will always be grateful for my first crush, back in the most indescribably awesome/awkward time of life known as sophomore year in high school. She made me want to be a better guy. I met her at a Saturday night dance and knew pretty much nothing about her except that she made my heart go boom. I thought, "Man, what if she's like, perfect? I'd better get my act together to be as perfect as I can be for her." I don't know what perfume she wore, but it was heavenly. I didn't wash my shirt from the dance because it smelled like her. I just kept it in my closet and sniffed it every once in a while. Yep, first real crush.

Well, the crush lasted all of five or six weeks, but those five or six weeks honestly changed my life because I acted on that desire to be a better person. I started opening doors for people. Saying hi to everyone. Smiling at them. Being a nice person. Stuff like that. I started doing the reading assignments in seminary. Reading the scriptures every day made them start to take on a whole new life to me. My prayers got more meaningful too. I started filling my mind with more thoughts of the Savior and His teachings and less of sports and music and stuff. This is when my testimony became my own. I became a much better person and, by no coincidence, a much happier person. And it all started because of this cute redhead who made me want to be a better person, even though she had no idea.

Seven years later, I met my wife. Not only did she make my heart go boom, she made me smile. Plus, she pretty much *was* perfect. I didn't have to speculate on that; I could see it. Oh man, now I really wanted to be a better person. I knew I had to up my game forever to be in this girl's league. I can honestly say that she has always inspired me to be a better person.

Your spouse should most definitely inspire you. If you don't want to be a better person by being around him or her, then you can't expect either one of you to grow. If he or she truly inspires you, odds are you have a keeper.

3. Does he or she make you laugh?

Remember the movie *Legacy*? David pries Eliza away from her fiancé because he doesn't make her laugh, and David does. You can't laugh without smiling. And you can't smile without being happy. The ability to laugh throughout life and sometimes at life is a huge insurance policy against marriage's challenges.

4. Does he or she make you happy?

Happiness is your ultimate goal out of all this. Don't forget that. "Men are that they might have joy" (2 Nephi 11:25). Don't forget to be happy, and don't forget to look for someone who makes you smile. If there's more drama than smiles, that is very unlikely to get better if you're married.

5. What if he or she is, you know, *weird*?

Hey, The Doors said it best—people are strange. It happens. But remember also what Arby's says—different is good. I agree wholeheartedly. I think a little bit of zaniness is a big plus. There are a lot of different people in the world, and they make the world a better place.

If you're not compatible because of a little too much zaniness or weirdness or whatever you want to call it, then you're not compatible.

That means you shouldn't pretend to be someone you're not, either. Be yourself, but as President Monson has taught, "be your best self" (*Be Your Best Self* [Salt Lake City: Deseret Book, 1979]).

Q: Don't these qualifications narrow the playing field too much? Aren't you telling us to look for a pretty-much-perfect person?

A: No, because remember, a major point of this book is to help us all improve.

We have recognized many times in this book that everybody needs to grow and change. Nobody is perfect. In fact, please teach your children that if they start looking for someone perfect, they will never get married. The imperfections we've discussed here can all be changed. They may not be likely to change from external forces (think: a spouse or girlfriend/boyfriend's influence), but *internal* forces (think: what we choose to do with ourselves) are a whole different story. We have complete control over ourselves. We can change, and hopefully this book will help more than one person change for the sake of becoming a better spouse, either now or in the future.

If you or your children are discouraged in the world of dating (or not dating), hang in there. I couldn't get a date in high school. I'm still not sure whether I was a geek or a nerd (okay, whether I *am* a geek or a nerd), but I was definitely *not* a jock or a hunk. I was worried for what seemed like forever at the time that I would never be able to find someone who would date me, much less marry me. I still ended up with a fantastic wife and beautiful children. Keep your head up. Blessings always await those who keep the commandments, but those blessings rarely come on our own timeline.

An Allegory to Apply
What You've Learned

I've hit lots of general questions and answers. I've gone deeply into the journey and talked about a whole lot of the most common threats. I've even gone into what we should teach our children to help them. In all of that, I've given a whole lot of clues about what to look for, and I've done it with an emphasis on the question that we have to ask ourselves constantly. You know it by now—"Lord, is it I?" What can *we* do to avoid these traps in ourselves and make sure we're part of the solution, not the problem?

Now I get the chance to put it all together with the help of an allegory. An allegory is basically a long parable—much like a fairy tale. Many parts of the allegory are symbols that come together to form a big theme and a powerful central message. For example, Jacob 5 is perhaps the best-known allegory in the scriptures, as it relates the history of the apostasy and restoration using a vineyard and the lord of the vineyard as the main symbols.

For additional reference, this whole book has been a sort of allegory, courtesy of the symbols in our fairy-tale theme. You remember those symbols. The prince is the husband. The princess is the wife. Marriage and the marriage covenant are the path to happily ever after, and eternity in the celestial kingdom is happily ever after.

The allegory we will learn from is actually a true story, a story of a modern-day ghost town that is filled with lessons both actual and symbolic that apply to lots of things in life, but especially to marriage. As we go through this unfortunately true tale, keep your eyes, heart, and mind open for lessons that apply to marriage. You will probably want to look specifically for many if not most of the pitfalls we've mentioned in this book.

On that note, I give you the allegory of Centralia.

Centralia, Pennsylvania, grew to prominence as a coal mining town. A cute little slice of rural-American life, Centralia reached its peak population of about 4,000 just before the 1900s. Although it was small, Centralia boasted an exceptional deposit of rich anthracite coal. This is high-quality coal that tends to be deposited in vertical veins. It burns very well and has been a staple of American energy for well over a century.

Our lesson on Centralia begins on Memorial Day, 1962. The residents of Centralia meet at a town council meeting on May 7 to discuss cleaning up the landfill in preparation for Memorial Day. They take their Memorial Day celebrations very seriously and want this to be a nice day. Cleaning up the landfill, one of a few places where residents have traditionally dumped their trash, is important because this particular site is next to the cemetery. The residents can't properly celebrate Memorial Day by decorating their cemetery appropriately when it's next to a messy dump.

The town council minutes do not discuss the proposed procedure to clean up the landfill. Some speculate that this is because state law prohibits dump fires in general, not just dump fires in or around any of Pennsylvania's numerous strip mines. State law also requires regular inspection of strip mine sites. The town council minutes seem to overlook these laws as they discuss the way to clean up the dump this Memorial Day.

On May 27, 1962, Centralia cleans up its dump by—you guessed it—burning the trash.

Visible flames are doused that night with water.

On May 29, 1962, flames are spotted again. Residents hook up garden hoses to try to douse this fire that has been smoldering for two days now.

On June 4, 1962, flames are spotted again. This time, a bulldozer heads into the pit to help get water to levels of the fire that had not been doused before. Shortly thereafter, a hole 15 feet wide and several feet tall is discovered in the pit.

By July 2, 1962, the local church complains of a stench from the pit. But residents continue to dump trash into the smoldering mess. It is still burning over a month later. The rich anthracite coal under Centralia has caught fire.

Later that summer, Gordon Smith, a mining engineer in nearby Pottsville, tells the town council he can dig out the fire for $175. The town refuses the offer. It's too expensive. They don't want to use $175 of the town's budget to put out the fire. It is rumored that a local resident, Alonzo Sanchez, also offers to use his backhoe to dig out the fire if he is permitted to keep the coal that he digs out with it. He is refused also, for various legal reasons and fear of greed. The residents don't want to give up any coal to Alonzo.

On August 6, 1962, with the fire still burning, the town council reluctantly sends the Lehigh Valley Coal Company formal notice of the fire, hoping to get some help extinguishing the fire. The town council is afraid to tell the LVCC how the fire really started because they believe the LVCC will not offer any help if they know that it was started illegally. The town claims the fire was "of unknown origin . . . During a period of unusually hot weather." At the ensuing meeting, representatives from the LVCC and Susquehanna Coal Company state they do not have the resources to put out the fire. The Deputy Secretary of Mines, James Shober, Sr., therefore announces that he expects the state to pick up the tab for digging out the fire.

On August 19, 1962, about three months after the fire started, a contract for digging out the fire is awarded to Bridy, Inc., the lowest bidder, for $20,000. The project runs out of money when Bridy, Inc. excavates more than twice the originally expected number of cubic yards and the fire is still not out. Bridy had vastly underestimated what would be necessary to dig out this fire and is not willing to sink any more lost money into the project.

On October 29, 1963, the project started by Bridy, Inc., resumes with an effort to flush out the fire with a mixture of water and crushed rock. This contract is awarded to the low bidder for $28,400. An additional $14,000 is later approved as money is running out quickly. Funding for the project runs out on March 15, 1963. The project is never finished.

On April 11, 1963, nearly a year after the fire started, it is observed to have spread 700 feet from its origin, as steam begins to plume from other holes in the ground.

On July 1, 1963, three more proposals are made for the next attempt. The first, costing $277,490, proposes entrenching the fire and backfilling the trench with incombustible material. The second, costing $151,714, offers to dig a smaller trench in a semicircle around the fire, followed by a flush barrier to complete the circle. The third, bid at $82,300, proposes to continue the flushing project from October. The state of Pennsylvania, tired of footing the bill, abandons the project and approves none of the proposals.

And Centralia continues to burn.

Vents are later installed to monitor the underground inferno as it continues to smolder.

Now we fast forward to February 14, 1981, nearly twenty years after the fire started. Twelve-year-old Todd Domboski is playing in his grandmother's backyard when the ground suddenly opens up beneath him and he falls into a pit. Todd grabs onto a tree root to keep from falling into the chasm and is quickly rescued by his fourteen-year-old cousin, Eric Wolfgang. Temperatures are observed to be over 300 degrees in the pit. Lethal levels of carbon monoxide are also observed in the pit. Somehow, Todd is not killed by either the pit, its baking temperatures, or the lethal gases oozing from the pit.

In May 1981, town residents pass an informal resolution stating that they are willing to tear down the whole town and relocate it.

On June 22, 1981, newspaper and magazine articles begin reporting on the Centralia fire. Surface temperatures in resident Joan Girolami's backyard are measured at a staggering 626 degrees Fahrenheit. Homes continue to crumble as the ground beneath them is literally consumed by fire.

The New York Times runs the story "Slow Burn in Centralia, PA," noting poor Todd Domboski's story.

Estimated costs for extinguishing the fire now run at $100 million, in 1981 dollars.

In these articles, some residents of Centralia complain that the government hasn't put out the fire for them. They lament having to wait—and wait in vain—for someone to rescue them from their slowly burning town. Apparently, these residents do not agree with, or are unaware of, the informal resolution of the town council to tear down what's left of the city and relocate everyone.

On November 21, 1981, local gas station owner and Centralia mayor, John Coddington, becomes concerned when he notices the gas in his underground tanks is unusually warm. The gas is measured to be 172 degrees Fahrenheit. Apparently, Centralia residents are not interested in finding out firsthand at what temperature this gasoline will combust. The gas station is torn down. With their mayor making this drastic decision, residents of Centralia continue to leave.

As Centralia's population continues to dwindle over the next few years, the town is condemned, and most of the few remaining residents are moved out.

Today, Centralia's population is seven.

Scientists estimate that the Centralia fire will continue to burn for another 250 years.

What Are the Symbols in This Allegory?

The residents of Centralia are you—husband, wife, and family.

The fire in Centralia represents all the threats along your path to happily ever after.

Now, What Lessons Did You Learn from Centralia?

You have now trained yourself to ask, "Lord, is it I?" You have also trained yourself to recognize all sorts of threats to a marriage, and you've compared those threats symbolically to all sorts of dangers. You should now be able to spot all sorts of symbolic threats in the story of Centralia and apply them.

What are they? You should have your own answers, but let me point out a few obvious ones.

Let me start with: Be careful taking out your trash! This whole fire started with a terrible way of taking out trash. In marriage, our "trash" can be our moments of frustration in everyday life. These end up being our unkind words, the mosquitoes that pester and kill like no other animal. Don't take out your trash on your spouse or your family.

We can probably phrase this a different way and say, "Don't be stupid." "O, be wise; what can I say more?" (Jacob 6:12).

How about, don't let things simmer? When there is a problem, don't let it fester. Forgive. Show mercy. Be honest in discussing the problem and coming up with a solution.

And obedience? The fire was started in violation of both law and advice that Centralia had received. Stay on the map. Keep your covenants. Be obedient to the laws of God.

And did you notice that their dishonesty didn't help, either? It made the town residents afraid to ask for proper help. When you've done something wrong, fess up.

How about self-reliance? Did you notice all the people sitting around waiting for the government to help them, when they could have helped themselves? This to me is one of the biggest themes of the story. It certainly is a big theme in the Church, so it certainly should be a big theme in a successful marriage. We can't sit around waiting for someone to rescue our marriage, to pay our debt, and so on. We have to be the ones to act.

Did you notice how much more expensive the problem continued to grow? They could have put it out easily at the beginning with just $175 or even for free if they had just let poor Alonzo keep the coal he dug out. Instead, it grew more and more expensive until finally it was beyond any cost to put out the fire. Put a prompt and early end to problems in marriage, lest they smolder and grow out of control.

Speaking of growing out of control, did you notice that not one person died in over fifty years of a burning town? To me, this is a lesson on the Lord's infinite mercy. Even with all of the terrible things that happened over decades, not one person died.

And what about perseverance? Marriages always require perseverance—in a good way, not in a stubborn way. Many efforts to put out the fire were abandoned. We'll never know if they would have worked because they were never finished.

Did you catch the part where vents were installed to "monitor" the progress of the fire? Did anybody realize what should have been pretty obvious, that these "vents" would just provide more oxygen for the fire to burn? What kinds of "vents" do we install in our own marriages that only feed the fire?

We've always known that two wrongs don't make a right, but how many wrongs did these people go through in trying to get it right? The same holds true for marriage.

This is not at all a complete list. Hopefully you will see many, many more lessons in the tragedy of Centralia. And hopefully you will apply those lessons in your own marriage, lest your marriage burn down and lest your home become a ghost town.

THE PARABLE OF EDELWEISS

And now, I'd like to bring us back to where we began. The first piece of advice offered in this book was the bold statement that there is no such thing as an unhappy couple who regularly and worthily attends the temple. From there, other pieces of advice centered around the temple and the importance of always being worthy of a temple recommend. With these pieces of advice in mind, I leave you with a parable.

A young Austrian boy grew up admiring a shy young girl with curls in her hair and a smile that brought her head just a little to the side and then down toward the ground whenever it appeared. This shy gesture grew on the boy, and he became determined to make this little girl smile, if for no other reason than his love for seeing her smile. As they grew up together, the boy's feelings grew as well. As a strapping teenage boy, he now felt something different about the girl's adorable shy smile. He no longer felt that it was just fun to see, for he now loved everything about the girl behind the smile. He now felt that it was time to tell this girl just how he felt about her. He didn't want just to tell her; he wanted to show her. By now, to be with this girl forever was all he wanted.

The boy knew of a flower growing high up on the steep and treacherous Austrian Alps. He knew that girls loved flowers, and this flower, the edelweiss, was the most beautiful and rare of all flowers. To pick such a flower for her would require him to risk his life climbing the mountain, but he knew that it would be the ultimate token of his love and devotion for the girl. He had spent years practicing his skills scaling the Alps, and he was now ready to put those skills to the test.

The boy climbed the mountain and began his search for this matchless white flower. When he found it, he was careful to protect it for the trip back down the mountain to present it to the girl. He knew that the flower did not live long after being picked, so he had to hurry, but most of all he had to be careful. He placed the edelweiss carefully and securely in a box for the trek back to the valley.

Upon arriving at the girl's home, the boy smiled, hardly containing his joy, with his hands behind his back holding a treasure. He revealed the flower, gently handed it to her, and humbly asked, "Will you marry me?" The smile he had loved for so many years was never as beautiful to him as it was at this very moment. "Yes," she lovingly whispered, with tears in her eyes.

What Are the Symbols in This Parable?

The boy and girl are obvious. They represent husband and wife.

Edelweiss is the token of pure and everlasting love.

The mountain where the edelweiss grows is the temple.

What Does It All Mean?

To give you a little more understanding, edelweiss means "noble white." White is a symbol for purity and also for victory. In edelweiss, we have nobility, purity, and victory—all fitting symbols and descriptions of a temple marriage. Through the ordinances of the temple, a husband and wife are blessed with the greatest nobility of all—becoming reborn sons and daughters of God and heirs to all that He has. Likewise, they can ultimately be pronounced perfectly and completely clean. That is the ultimate victory over all the villains and other threats on the path to happily ever after.

Edelweiss only grows on mountains, high above the pollution and far above the valley floor, at an elevation of between 5,900 and 9,800 feet. The symbolism of a mountain is the key to this parable. Mountains are the closest place to heaven on earth. They are the perfect scriptural symbol for the temple. The nobility and purity of edelweiss is only found in the temple. The purity and nobility that define a celestial marriage can only grow in the environment of the temple and temple worthiness.

Edelweiss does not live very long after it is picked. To keep the flower in fresh supply in our homes down in the valley, we have to return frequently to the mountain.

Notice that our young man was careful to protect the edelweiss on the trip back down the mountain. Righteous priesthood holders are careful to protect the purity of their loved ones in the same way.

In this parable, edelweiss stands as a token of love, purity, and nobility. Our young man risked his life to present his sweetheart with this token of his love. A token is shared between two people as physical proof of their agreement. In temple terms, we call that agreement a covenant. The token of this covenant is only to be shared between a husband and wife within the boundaries of marriage.

Finally, our young man was willing to risk his life to climb that mountain to pick the edelweiss. Some Austrian boys do indeed fall to their deaths trying to pick edelweiss. Perhaps this carries a lesson of being fully prepared and worthy to enter the temple. Our young man spent years honing his climbing skills before he made his climb. Growing up in a righteous home, our children have the blessing and advantage of spending years of being worthy to enter the temple before making the edelweiss climb. If we give our children this blessing, then they will indeed be ready to make this climb.

And live happily ever after.

"There is nothing for me but to love you."

—Tony Bennett

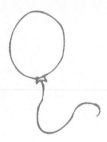

ACKNOWLEDGMENTS

Thank you so much to the outstanding staff at Cedar Fort! Thank you also to Norma Smiley for the great help editing the manuscript and bouncing ideas off of.

Thank you to my father for his wonderful example of a great husband.

Thank you to Cami for letting me gush about you publicly and for standing by me.

And thank you in advance to Jamison, Jaren, and my future sons-in-law for taking care of Heidi, Kayla, Claire, Anna, and Robyn and getting them back home safely and happily to their Father in Heaven.

ABOUT THE AUTHOR

Mark Shields has been happily married to his wife, Cami, since 1992. They are the proud parents of five daughters—Heidi, Kayla, Claire, Anna, and Robyn—and one son-in-law, Jamison. He practices as an attorney in Mesa, Arizona, where the family has lived since 2001. He has competed in a number of races, including the 2015 Boston Marathon, and enjoys building high-quality speakers and other stereo equipment in his spare time. He's served in many capacities, including bishop; temple and missionary preparation instructor; Primary, nursery, seminary, and Sunday School teacher; high councilor; and temple worker.

Scan to visit

markshieldsauthor.com